Jane Arnold • Zoltán Dörnyei • Chaz Pugliese

THE PRINCIPLED COMMUNICATIVE APPROACH
Seven Criteria for Success

HELBLING
LANGUAGES

The Principled Communicative Approach
by Jane Arnold, Zoltán Dörnyei and Chaz Pugliese
© HELBLING LANGUAGES 2015

First published 2015
ISBN 978-3-85272-938-1

Content edited by Thomas Strasser
Copy edited by Jill Florent
Designed by Giorgia Probani
Cover design by Capolinea
Printed by Bieffe

Every effort has been made to trace the owners of any copyright material in this book.

If notified, the publisher will be pleased to rectify any errors or omissions.

Contents

Contents

What is the Principled Communicative Approach?

In writing this book, we have been guided by two convictions. First, we believe that modern language instruction in general should follow broadly communicative principles, which is how Communicative Language Teaching (CLT) has traditionally been understood. Second, we also believe that CLT, which was originally launched in the 1970s, could do with some revitalisation in order to make it more fitting for the 21st century. There have been considerable developments in applied and psycholinguistics since the turn of the new millennium, and these should be reflected in the way we conceive and then put into practice communicative principles. The most important theoretical advances in this area were described by Zoltán in his 2009 book, *The Psychology of Second Language Acquisition* (especially in the final chapter, "The Psychology of Instructed Second Language Acquisition"), and he summed up the practical implications of his findings in seven broad principles, each of which was based on scientific considerations (see Dörnyei, 2013). Zoltán referred to this upgrade of CLT as the "Principled Communicative Approach", and the main objective of the current volume is to bring this approach to life by offering a range of practical classroom activities that embody the seven principles.

Why do we need a new approach to CLT?

Over the past decades CLT has become a cornerstone of language teaching methodology, but curiously, the specific content of the teaching approach has remained rather elusive. As Littlewood (2011: 541) pointed out, "A recurrent comment about communicative language teaching is that nobody knows what it is". This curious situation was not the result of classroom practitioners failing to keep up with scholarly guidelines, but rather the absence of any authoritative guidelines. Indeed, Richards and Rodgers (2001: 155) have been right to point out about CLT that "There is no single text or authority on it, nor any single model that is universally accepted as authoritative". We should also add that this vagueness is not a new phenomenon regarding CLT. Ever since the genesis of the method in the early 1970s, its proponents have developed a very wide range of variants that were only loosely related to each other. This was caused – as we shall see below – by the fact that while CLT had a firm and elaborate linguistic foundation, the psychological understanding of how to convey the linguistic content was rather imprecise. Therefore, while language teaching experts and materials writers became increasingly clear about what linguistic aspects of the second/foreign language (L2) to focus on, there were no firm guidelines on *how* best to present and teach this language content. It is fair to say that before the turn of the millennium there was no attempt to bring CLT in line with the theoretical advances of the psychology of learning in general and second language acquisition in particular. This underdeveloped psychological dimension inevitably led to diverse practical interpretations, of which the best-known example is the disagreement among experts about how to teach *grammar*. Before we present our proposal for reform, let us take a brief tour of the historical development of CLT, as this will allow us to indicate where the roots of the current confusion are.

A brief history of Communicative Language Teaching

Communicative language teaching was introduced at the beginning of the 1970s by British and American scholars to promote the teaching of communicative skills in modern language education, and especially in the teaching of English as a global language. Although the method was seen by many as a counterreaction to the audiolingual method that dominated the field in the 1960s, the main goal of CLT – to develop functional communicative L2 competence – was not unlike the primary audiolingual objective. However, CLT pursued the communicative agenda in a radically different manner from its predecessor: instead of trying to build up L2 knowledge through techniques inspired by behaviourism such as drilling and rote learning, CLT methodology was centred around authentic communication. The emphasis was on the learner's participatory experience in meaningful L2 interaction in (often simulated) communicative situations, which was seen as essential for preparing them for future communication in real-life contexts. The approach underscored the significance of designing less structured and more creative language tasks with as many authentic elements as possible. For this reason, the traditional processing of scripted coursebook dialogues was replaced by games, problem-solving tasks, discussions and unscripted situational role-play activities, and the infamous hallmark of audiolingualism, pattern drilling, was either completely abandoned or was replaced by 'communicative drills'. As a result, the communicative L2 classroom became a potentially more stimulating and less cognitively dull environment than the typical learning context associated with audiolingualism (let alone grammar-translation).

From a theoretical point of view, the difference between the audiolingual approach and CLT was one of orientation. Audiolingualism was associated with a specific *learning theory* – adapted from behaviourist psychology– and was therefore the first language teaching method that consciously aspired to build on the principles of the psychology of learning. In contrast, the communicative reform in the 1970s was motivated by developments in modern linguistics. When some of the shortcomings of the original CLT proposals became obvious in the 1990s, most attempts for improvement concentrated on strengthening the linguistic foundation of the method. This trend was well reflected in Nina Spada's (2007: 271) summary:

> 'most second language educators agree that CLT is undergoing a transformation – one that includes increased recognition of and attention to language form within exclusively or primarily meaning-oriented CLT approaches to second language instruction'.

It was in this vein that Marianne Celce-Murcia, Zoltán Dörnyei and Sarah Thurrell (1997, 1998) first introduced the concept of a "principled communicative approach" (PCA) in the second half of the 1990s. This involved extending the systematic treatment of language issues traditionally restricted to sentence-bound rules (i.e. grammar) to the explicit development of other knowledge areas and skills necessary for efficient communication. Drawing on a number of theoretical strands such as Austin and Searle's *speech act theory*, Dell Hymes' model of *communicative competence* and its application to L2 proficiency by

Canale and Swain, as well as Halliday's *systemic functional grammar*, they proposed detailed checklists for each of the main facets of communicative competence and argued that these components should be systematically and directly targeted by CLT tasks.

Looking back, the proposed linguistic fine-tuning pointed in the right direction, but as we have seen, it lacked a crucial element: complementing the linguistic innovations with a matching psychological conception of L2 learning. Indeed, the only learning-specific 'principle' that was available for CLT materials developers and practitioners was the broad and rather vague tenet of *learning through doing*, coupled with the only marginally less ambiguous guideline of developing the learners' communicative competence through *seeking situational meaning*. Scholars used these terms widely and people seemed to understand their main gist, but in retrospect we can say that the exact meaning of these terms was never explicitly explained or operationalized. Instead, the general conception underlying learning within a CLT framework was confined to the widespread assumption that learners' communicative competence develops automatically through active participation in meaningful communicative tasks. This made intuitive sense; after all, children master their first language this way, so what could go wrong? As it turned out, quite a lot. Let us illustrate the various dilemmas in CLT by looking at two central aspects of the method: the development of grammar and fluency.

Grammar and the implicit/explicit learning dichotomy

Many followers of CLT have tended to associate the method with a basically 'no-grammar' or at least 'not-a-lot-of-grammar' approach, epitomised by Krashen's (1982) *Input Hypothesis*, which downplayed the conscious teaching of grammatical rules and foregrounded the provision of meaningful, comprehensible input as the driving force of effective L2 instruction. The argument was that because children do not focus on grammar as they acquire their L1, a strong emphasis on grammar is not essential, and can even be distracting, as far as the development of communicative skills are concerned. This position gained support from the recognition that in real-life communication grammatical accuracy is not essential – after all, does it really matter if we get a tense wrong as long as we are understood?

Other CLT proponents, however, disagreed with this view, and interestingly this group included most of the founding fathers and mothers of the method. If we re-read the early documents of the communicative approach, we find that most of the original CLT theoreticians were quite keen to emphasize salient structural linguistic components, as illustrated, for example, by the initial sentence of Littlewood's highly influential teaching methodology text – *Communicative Language Teaching: An Introduction* (1981): "One of the most characteristic features of communicative language teaching is that it pays systematic attention to functional as well as structural aspects of language, combining these into a more fully communicative view." Not only did this group of scholars not think that including grammar would undermine the effectiveness of communicative language teaching, they believed that a focus on accuracy was an essential part of the method.

What is the Principled Communicative Approach?

These contrasting stances regarding grammar corresponded to a well-known psychological dichotomy, that of *implicit* versus *explicit learning*. *Explicit learning* refers to the learner's conscious and deliberate attempt to master some material or solve a problem. This is the learning type emphasized by most school instruction. In contrast, *implicit learning* involves acquiring skills and knowledge without conscious awareness, that is, automatically and often with no intentional attempt to learn them. Naturalistic language acquisition (e.g. picking up a language while staying in the host environment) clearly falls under this latter category, and as we saw earlier, the emerging view of a typical communicative classroom was that it should approximate a naturalistic learning context as closely as possible, thereby providing plenty of authentic input to feed the students' implicit learning processors. Undoubtedly, this view was to a large extent motivated by the fact that the main language learning model for humans – the mastery of our mother tongue – predominantly involves implicit processes without any explicit teaching; quite amazingly, children acquire the incredibly complex system of their L1 entirely through engaging in natural and meaningful communication with their parents and other caretakers, without receiving any tuition whatsoever, not even systematic corrective feedback. The implicit nature of this process is evidenced by the fact that most people cannot explain the rules of their mother tongue once they have mastered them.

Relying on the implicit learning model that nature has provided would indeed be a comfortable and straightforward solution when mastering an L2. Unfortunately, however, while implicit language processing does a great job in generating native-speaking L1 proficiency in children, it does not seem to work efficiently later when we want to acquire an additional language within institutional contexts. Unguided learning through mere exposure to natural language input does not seem to lead to sufficient progress in L2 attainment for most school-age and adult learners! This was demonstrated very clearly by the accumulated experiences in immersion programmes – seen by many as an instructional approach that offers optimal conditions for implicit L2 learning – which indicated that immersion school students generally fail to acquire native–like proficiency in the L2. Accordingly, most scholars gradually came to agree with Lightbown and Spada's (2006: 176) conclusion that "we do not find support for the hypothesis that language acquisition will take care of itself if second language learners simply focus on meaning in comprehensible input".

If relying on implicit learning is not the answer, we are left with the alternative option that for best effect, L2 language learning needs to be scaffolded by some form of focused explicit instruction. The crucial question is how this scaffolding can be achieved without jeopardizing the benefits of the communicative approach. It is not a question of advocating a back-to-grammar-translation method, so the challenge is to find ways of maximizing the *cooperation* between explicit and implicit learning. Finding a theoretically sound and practically achievable response has been the main motivation behind developing the Principled Communicative Approach.

What is the Principled Communicative Approach?

Communicative fluency

Everybody who has ever tried to speak in a foreign language knows that the accurate use of linguistic form is not the only, and very often not the most serious, concern with regard to communicative effectiveness. In many respects, *communicative fluency* is more significant and the implicit-explicit dichotomy discussed above also plays a crucial role in understanding this aspect of communication. In the literature of the psychology of language learning, fluency is usually discussed under the broader concept of "automaticity/automatization", and the promotion of fluency is usually subsumed under "skill learning theory". Thus, from a psychological point of view the relevant issue to explore is how L2 skills can be automatized.

Let us briefly look at the main tenets of *skill learning theory* because they illustrate how both explicit and implicit processes are necessary for the successful mastery of L2 communicative competence. Skill learning theory holds that the automatization of any skill, including language skills, requires implicit – or *procedural* – knowledge. Although this theory is consistent with Krashen's (1982) proposal that communicative competence relies on implicit (acquired) knowledge, it contradicts Krashen's theory by positing that in order to build up an implicit knowledge base, one has to start out by receiving explicit knowledge. The development of any skill (driving, knitting, playing tennis, etc.) needs to start with some initial explicit – or *declarative* – input, which in turn becomes gradually *automatized* through repetition. Thus, even though the ultimate goal of skill-learning is to arrive at automatized, implicit knowledge, a systematically designed fluency-building sequence is made up of an initial explicit teaching stage and subsequent practice, further divided into *controlled* and *open-ended* practice:

1   The *declarative input stage* provides clear and concise rules as well as sufficient examples that the learner can then interpret and rehearse, to raise explicit awareness of the skill to be internalized.

2   The *controlled practice stage* should offer opportunities for abundant repetition within a narrow context. "Narrow" is a key attribute here because the proceduralization of explicit knowledge requires a great deal of repetition, not unlike the way a musician practises a piece again and again. Therefore, the key to the effectiveness of this stage is to design drills that are engaging rather than demotivating.

3   The *open-ended practice stage* involves the continuous improvement in the performance of a skill that is already well established in a more varied and less structured applicability range.

Skill-learning theory has been validated by extensive psychological research (see DeKeyser and Criado, 2013a; Dörnyei, 2009), and interestingly, the sequence of *declarative input* → *controlled practice* → *open-ended practice* is reminiscent of the well-known methodological progression of *presentation* → *practice* → *production* (PPP).

The seven main principles of the Principled Communicative Approach (PCA)

The previous discussion has indicated that the real challenge for language teaching methodology in the 21st century is to specify the nature of the optimal cooperation between explicit and implicit learning processes in a systematic manner. Working out all the details of a new, principled communicative approach is clearly an ongoing process, but we can formulate some key guiding principles for the approach. Dörnyei (2009) offered seven maxims, which are in accordance with the state of the art of current psycholinguistic research:

1   *The personal significance principle*: the PCA should be meaning-focused and personally significant. This has been the basic tenet of student-centred, communicative language teaching and we believe that this principle is just as valid now as when it was first formulated.

2   *The declarative input principle*: To facilitate automatization, the PCA should involve explicit initial input components that are then 'proceduralized' through practice.

3   *The controlled practice principle*: While the overall aim of CLT is to prepare learners for meaningful communication, skill learning theory suggests that the PCA should also include controlled practice activities to promote the automatization of L2 skills.

4   *The focus on form principle*: While maintaining an overall meaning-oriented approach, the PCA should also pay attention to the formal/structural aspects of the L2 that determine accuracy and appropriateness at the sentence, discourse and pragmatic levels.

5   *The formulaic language principle*: the PCA should include the teaching of formulaic language (e.g. fixed expressions, idioms, set phrases, collocations) as a featured component. There should be sufficient awareness raising of the significance and the pervasiveness of formulaic language in real-life communication, and selected phrases should be practised and recycled intensely.

6   *The language exposure principle*: the PCA should offer extensive exposure to large amounts of L2 input that can feed the learners' implicit learning mechanisms. In order to make the most of this exposure, learners should be given some explicit preparation in terms of pre-task activities, to prime them for maximum intake.

7   *The focused interaction principle*: the PCA should offer learners ample opportunities to participate in genuine L2 interaction. For best effect, such communicative practice should always have a specific formal or functional focus, and should always be associated with target phrases to practise.

Each of these principles will be explored in a separate chapter, starting with a brief theoretical overview and then presenting practical ideas on how to implement the principles in classroom tasks. Let us conclude this introduction by reiterating that the essence of the Principled Communicative Approach is the integration of meaningful communication with relevant declarative input and the automatization of both linguistic rules and lexical items. By applying the right principles to teaching L2 skills we can significantly increase in the effectiveness of the learning process.

CHAPTER 1
THE PERSONAL SIGNIFICANCE PRINCIPLE

Introduction

In the introduction of their influential teachers' resource book, *Grammar in Action*, Christine Frank and Mario Rinvolucri (1991:16) wrote the following:

> If we consider the students in our classes to be more interesting than the rather cardboard characters found in the traditional course book, it follows that a real need exists for activities where the students are invited to speak to each other and express their ideas using structures that have already been presented to them. Practising structures in this very personal series of contexts is much more emotionally real than practising them in the make-belive world of a textbook.

This quote expresses the essence of an educational orientation – often referred to as 'student-centred learning' – which places the student rather than the teacher or the teaching material at the heart of the educational process. Drawing on principles originally developed in educational psychology by experts such as Maria Montessori and Carl Rogers, CLT adopted right from its genesis a student-centred approach that tried to engage learners as "real" people rather than occupiers of student roles. This "realness" has been described in several ways, for example as 'congruence', 'authenticity' or the engagement of 'transportable identities', and it presupposes that students are not viewed as being empty vessels to be filled with information by the teacher but rather as responsible agents who take ownership of their learning. The main role of teachers in this respect is to act as facilitators in promoting *genuine* learning, which is viewed as a function of the students' active construction of their own meaning based on the interactions they have with each other and the resources at their disposal. As Carl Rogers (1965: 389) said, "I know I cannot teach anyone anything, I can only provide an environment in which he can learn".

As we pointed out earlier, a fundamental motivation behind developing CLT had been to depart from the mechanical drilling or the memorization of soulless texts in audiolingualism, and to place instead meaning-focused and personally relevant communication between real people at the centre of the classroom activity. In her classic book, *Caring and Sharing in the Foreign Language Class*, Gertrude Moskowitz (1978: 197) summarized this tenet very clearly:

> By connecting the content with the students' lives, you are focusing on what students know rather than what they are ignorant of. From the learner's standpoint, there is quite a psychological difference in dealing with what is familiar to him rather than what is unknown. Start where the students are – concentrating on areas of their daily lives in which they have thoughts, reactions, and experience. In foreign language teaching, we customarily begin with the lives of others, with whom students may not easily identify, and then expect students to transfer the material to their own lives. However, transfer to the textbook is easier when the content starts with the student himself and then leads into the materials to be learned.

This striving to make language learning personally meaningful – *personal significance principle* – is, we believe, just as valid now as it was when CLT first emerged, and the following activities are intended to illustrate the potential range of this approach.

What's in a poem?

Focus	Personal responses to a poem
Level	Upper intermediate and above
Time	25-30 minutes
Preparation	Make copies or prepare a slide of the poem.

in class

1 Hand out the poem below or have it on a slide.

2 Let the students read the poem silently. Clear up any doubts they have about vocabulary.

3 Ask them to experiment individually with their voice: read it loudly, softly, quickly, slowly.

4 Now ask them to consider the following questions in small groups:

> How did the poet feel when he wrote the poem? What makes you say so?
> Who do you think the poem was written for?
> What metaphors are being used? Are they effective?

5 Now ask the students to think of a period in their life in "black and white", and one in "Technicolor".

6 For homework ask them to write a poem about something related to their lives.

7 In the next class, collect the students' poems and stick them on the walls. Invite the students to walk around and read what everyone has written and to comment on the poems with each other. Encourage reactions like: *I liked Maria's poem because… Jaime's poem surprised/frightened me because…*

In Stereo where Available

My life was dust and scratches
Missing frames, poorly enacted
Reel after reel
Silent

I was a faded projection
In a seedy forgotten theatre
A battered clown
Merely waiting for The End

Enter third act, you
A bulb enlightment
Twenty-four times per second
Redeeming

My life was Glorious Black and White
You turned it Technicolor
Full Cinemascope
In Stereo where available

Eugene Sanders (Atlanta, GA, 1970)

1.2 How would it be at home?

Focus Comparing coursebook material to students' own lives

Level Lower intermediate and above

Time 15-20 minutes

Preparation Choose a text or dialogue (e.g. from your coursebook) that describes an everyday scene/situation.

in class

1. Present the selected text/dialogue to the students. Explain to them that although they might find the scene/situation familiar, it would not coincide exactly with their home environment. You might illustrate with examples you are familiar with.

2. Ask the students – either as homework or as a writing task in class – to prepare a new, personalized version of the text imagining how the same situation would take place in their home context. Ask them to make it as personal as possible without adding any factual details (e.g. proper names) that might indicate who the author is.

3. Collect the new versions and then distribute them randomly, making sure that nobody gets their own.

4. Students read out the version they have been given, and the other students try to guess who the author was. Each time after several guesses, ask the authors to raise their hands. This can be done as a competition or used as the basis for a lively classroom discussion.

1.3 Routines

Focus	Adverbs of frequency with habits and routines
Level	Lower intermediate and above
Time	15-20 minutes
Preparation	None

in class

1 Ask the students to list a few routines they perform. Explain that you would like them to write full sentences with these routines using adverbs of frequency. Provide a model; for example: *I always read the news in the morning, I usually go for a run in the evening, I often have a glass of milk before I go to bed, I always shake hands when I meet my colleagues in the morning.*

2 Now ask them to look back at their list of routines and decide whether their routines are *choices* (things you do after thinking about them), or *habits* (behaviour we have repeated so much it has become almost involuntary).

3 Invite students to work in pairs and compare what they have written.

4 Now hold a plenary discussion. Have a few questions ready. For example: Is brushing your teeth in the morning or before going to bed a choice or a habit? Or also: Can a habit become a choice? (There might be some overlapping, as is often the case when we discuss categories, but this usually generates some talk).

1.4

I'm good at this!

Focus	*I'm good at + -ing*
Level	Elementary and above
Time	20-25 minutes
Preparation	None

in class

1 Begin by talking about two or three things you're good at:
I'm good at playing the guitar, I'm good at learning languages, I'm good at playing tennis.

2 Write the sentences on the board and ask the students what they notice.

3 Go over the rule, i.e., that the expression *I'm good at...* if followed by a verb will be verb + *-ing*.

4 Now ask the students to think of three things they think they're good at and write them down on a piece of paper.

5 Ask students to work in pairs and tell each other the things they have thought of.

6 Now collect their pieces of paper. With the students' permission, explain that you would like to pick a few at random, read them out and ask the class whether they could guess who wrote which. The author then answers any questions classmates may have.

Variations

For more advanced students go back to your examples. Tell them you'd like to give them more information. For example: *I'm good at playing the guitar because I practise every day. I'm good at learning languages because I enjoy talking to people from different countries.* Ask them to do the same for their three sentences. Leave them time to think about what they want to say. They give their information either in pairs or with the whole class.

1.5 Read all about me

Focus	Writing: An article about your life in the future
Level	Intermediate and above
Time	30-40 minutes
Preparation	None

in class

1 Tell students to do the following, pausing between each sentence: *Think about what things you would like to do in the future... Imagine several years have passed and you have done a lot of things in your life... See where you live... What work you have... What activities you do in your free time... What new skills you have developed...*

2 Ask students to take brief notes on what they imagined, writing down as many things as they can remember.

3 Then tell them: You are going to pretend that it is now that moment in the future and that the newspaper in the area where you live is publishing articles each day about people living there. Write the article about yourself that you would like to see in the newspaper. As a guideline, they can structure this using the following aspects:

> Your early life, schooling
> Your professional activity
> Hobbies and interests
> Personal qualities
> Contributions to the community

4 Ask students to write a first draft in class and then take it home to elaborate a bit more and finish. In the next class collect the students' articles and correct any important mistakes before handing them back for students to rewrite.

5 Decide on a way to "publish" the articles: make a booklet with a photocopy of each article, put each article on the walls for students to walk around the room and read or make a book which can be uploaded to the school web page or wiki.

1.6 Your town, my town, our town

Focus	Speaking: Preparing a presentation for visitors to your town
Level	Lower intermediate and above
Time	10-20 minutes a day for several days for presentations and 40 minutes after the presentations are finished
Preparation	Bring in a map of the town/city where your school is.

in class

1   Bring a map of the town/city where you have class. Individually, students will choose one place they personally like and at home will prepare a three- to five-minute presentation of the place, giving general information about it and explaining why they chose that place, what meaning it has for them. If possible, each should choose a different place.

2   During the next week or two to begin each class a few students give their presentations. They might use PowerPoint or bring in photos if they want.

3   When all have finished their presentations, the students in groups, preferably with people who have chosen places to describe in different parts of the city, prepare a good itinerary for visitors: what is most important to see, in what order, where might visitors stop for lunch, what time of the year would be best, and so forth.

4   Each group presents their itinerary to the class.

1.7 Personal strategies for learning

Focus	Developing personalized learning strategies
Level	Any
Time	In one class, 15-20 minutes. In class a week later 20-30 minutes
Preparation	Make a copy of the worksheet for each student.

in class

1   Explain to your students that there is no one best way to learn a language and that what is most helpful is for each person to find their own best way.

2   Give students a few examples of strategies people might use to learn a language and tell them it can help their learning to reflect on what helps them to learn the language, on how they like to learn and on what is most difficult for them in learning and what doesn't help them to learn.

3   Give each student a copy of the worksheet below. Tell them that during the next week they are going to think about their language learning and write some notes. They will then discuss anything they observed in small groups.

4   Remind students several times during the week to add comments. On the day set to discuss what they have written ask them to work in groups of three or four and compare comments, suggesting that they may find out new ways of learning from others in their group. For lower levels both in the writing and the discussing you may want to let them use their L1 at some points because developing and sharing strategies that are useful for them personally in their learning is an important aspect of this activity.

5   When students have had time to discuss their ideas, ask if anyone would like to share what things are most difficult for them and ask the class for any suggestions they might have, giving some of your own if necessary. For example, if one says they can't remember so many new words, you could suggest they make little flash cards to review the new words.

1.7 Personal strategies for learning

6   Encourage students to use any useful ideas they have received from this activity to improve their learning process.

What helps me to learn the language
How I like to learn
What is most difficult for me in learning the language
What doesn't help me to learn

Note

Although many students may not be used to reflecting in this way, reflection is an important part of any learning process and can help them to develop strategies for more effective learning. Having something to fill in and then discuss with classmates can make reflection more focussed and accessible.

1.8 Goal + effort = success

Focus	Listening and speaking: Setting goals for learning
Level	Lower intermediate and above
Time	40-50 minutes
Preparation	Find a video prepared where people talk about reaching goals. (See below for one suggestion). Make a copy of the worksheet for each student.

in class

1 Tell your students that they are going to practise listening comprehension and play them a video on setting goals. Ask them to try to remember the main points.

2 Discuss with them the importance of setting goals related to what we want to achieve and making plans of action about how to reach them.

3 Ask students to work individually for a few minutes writing down any reasons they can think of for why English could be useful for them in their future. Then ask them to think of one goal they have related to learning English. Tell them it should not be "to learn English" as working with goals on this level should be with sub-goals, e.g. to understand songs in English, to be able to communicate with people in English when travelling, etc. While they are writing, walk around the class and help any students who are having trouble thinking of a goal by asking them questions about what they like to do, what they would like to do in the future and pointing out any ways that knowing English might be useful to them.

4 When all the students have a goal, ask them to think of answers to the questions on the worksheet and write them down.

5 Ask students to work in pairs or groups of three and share their answers to the questions. Telling others about your goals can provide stronger motivation for taking action.

What is my goal?
Why is it important for me?
What things can I do to help me reach my goal?
What problems might I have and how could I solve them?

1.8 Goal + effort = success

Video on goal-setting

http://www.mindtools.com/page6.html

Variations

After Step 3, do a short visualization activity such as this: In a quiet voice say to your students: *Close your eyes or look down... Relax a moment and imagine you have achieved your goal... See yourself in the future when your goal is a reality... What changes are there in your life... How do you feel now that you have achieved your goal?... Enjoy seeing yourself having arrived at your goal... Now come back to the present but bring with you the idea that you can reach your goal if you work to do so...*

For more advanced students you could use a slide share to work in more depth with SMART goals: http://www.slideshare.net/emurfield/goal-setting-9227739

If you can't project the videos, give them a copy of the text from a link such as this or prepare a synthesis for them: http://www.mindtools.com/pages/article/newHTE_90.htm

Note

Markus and Ruvolo (1989) have worked with the concept of possible selves, the idea of who we might become, and they explain that 'imaging one's own actions through the construction of elaborated possible selves achieving the desired goal may thus directly facilitate the translation of goals into intentions and instrumental actions'. For more about the role of ideal selves in language learning see Dörnyei and Kubanyiova (2014) and Hadfield and Dörnyei (2013).

1.9 A conditional weekend

Focus	First conditional
Level	Lower intermediate and above
Time	40-50 minutes
Preparation	Make three copies of the weekend timetable for each pair of students.

in class

1 Review the first conditional, including examples such as the following:

   f we go to the park, we can take our lunch.
   If we go to the park, we will have time to relax/ we won't study.
   If we take our books, we can study in the park.

2 Ask students to work in pairs and give each pair three copies of the timetable. Each student writes down individually things they would like to do in some of the spaces, using the infinitive of the verbs: *go to the cinema, visit a friend...* You can specify how many activities to include perhaps five or six, and tell them that some activities may need more than one space so they can write these in two spaces.

3 Ask students to compare their timetables with their partner and plan to do things together. They will discuss this using the first conditional. Give them some examples; *If we go to the cinema on Friday evening, we can't go to the party. If we don't go to the concert on Sunday evening, we'll have time to study for our exam.*

4 Ask students to prepare a short dialogue about their weekend plans using the conditionals. Tell them to try to make it sound as natural as possible. An example to show them:

   A   *If we go to the cinema on Friday, we can't go to the party.*
   B   *Yes, but if we don't go to the cinema, we won't have time to see the new French film this week.*
   A   *You're right. But if we go to the cinema, we'll have to tell Alice we won't be at the party.*

1.9 A conditional weekend

5   Each pair presents their dialogue to the class.

	Friday	Saturday	Sunday
17:00-19:00			
19:00-20:00			
20:00-22:00			
22:00-24:00			

Acknowledgement

We learned a version of this activity from Taylor Winn.

1.10 Bring the past to the present

Focus	Writing: an account of someone's life in the past
Level	Lower intermediate and above
Time	10-15 minutes
Preparation	Choose a text about someone remembering their life in the past.

in class

1   Review the ways to talk about the past. Ask students to read a text about someone remembering the past or tell them about the person, emphasizing the examples of the past tenses which are used.

2   Ask students to think of a grandparent or someone older than them that they know (perhaps a neighbour, a friend's grandparent etc.) and that they could talk to in order to ask them about their life in the past. Ask students to prepare questions to ask about things that are interesting to them, that they would like to know more about. Tell them they will have a week to interview the person about the past, taking notes about the most interesting parts. They should ask the person for their permission to use the information in a composition they will write for class.

3   Ask students to write a composition in English with the information from the person they interviewed. Collect the compositions, correct the mistakes and ask the students to prepare a final version.

4   Decide with them on ways to share their work; for example photocopy and make a booklet, post the compositions on the walls for the class to read or perhaps on a class wiki, prepare posters that can be displayed in the school, etc.

1.11

What about you?

Focus	Expressing personal opinions
Level	Lower intermediate and above
Time	25-30 minutes
Preparation	None

in class

1   Ask students to write down five statements that express their personal opinion about things they feel strongly about. For example, *I really dislike adverts on TV.*

2   Their task, then, is to go around in the classroom, share their views with their classmates and then ask them: *"What about you?"*

3   For each statement they should record how many people agreed and how many disagreed.

4   Once they have talked to everybody, students share their findings with the class by reading out their statements and then the number of their classmates that agreed and disagreed with them..

1.12 From the composer's point of view

Focus	Imagining how an artist feels about their creation
Level	Lower intermediate and above
Time	20-30 minutes
Preparation	Choose a recording of a piece of instrumental music which your students probably aren't familiar with. One example which works well is Satie's *Gymnopedie 1*. Make a copy of the task sheet for each student.

in class

1 Play the music once. Explain to the students you just want them to listen and pay attention to the various features of the music (e.g. the instruments, whether it's loud or quiet, fast or slow, etc.).

2 Elicit a few reactions but don't spend too much time on this at this stage.

3 Hand out the task sheet on the next page. Tell students to imagine they wrote the music and have them complete the sentences. Play the music a second time in the background as they work.

4 Ask students to work in pairs and read each other's sentences.

5 If you have an internet connection in the classroom, go to Wikipedia so that the students can read up on Satie to see if there is anything there that justifies their answers.

Variations

The same exercise can be used with a picture of a work of art, a poem or a story.

1.12 From the composer's point of view

1) I wrote this piece of music because…

2) I hope I've achieved…

3) I'm pleased with…

4) I chose this title because…

5) It took me … to write this

6) When I was composing this, I was feeling…

7) When I finished this, I felt… because…

CHAPTER 1: THE PERSONAL SIGNIFICANCE PRINCIPLE

CHAPTER 2
THE DECLARATIVE INPUT PRINCIPLE

Introduction

Of the seven principles underlying the PCA, the *declarative input principle* will probably sound most familiar to teachers, because contemporary school practices involve a great deal of providing learners with initial explicit input in the form of facts, rules, information, L2 resources, etc. This process is, in fact, what many people would associate with 'teaching' in the traditional sense. While we argued earlier that students should not be seen as empty vessels that need to be filled with input, skill learning theory is very clear about the necessity of the initial encoding of a targeted skill, prior to any practice sessions, in the form of declarative knowledge. After all, everybody would agree that learning to drive should start with a theoretical part, and even before children start experimenting with cycling, parents often give them detailed instructions on what to do and what not. Psychological research as a whole is in agreement with such folk beliefs as it has been consistently shown that the initial stage of skill-building typically requires some kind of explicit element to provide relevant information and guidelines about the skill so that the learner/trainee can develop a rough mental approximation of it that can then be put to the test. The most effective method tends not to throw learners into the deep water to see if they sink or swim, but rather to prepare them for the task in a number of ways, most notably through verbal (or written) instruction or explanation, as well as by modelling the skill through a demonstration (perhaps with accompanying commentary), through examples, or by analogy with an existing skill. Thus, to provide a jump start for subsequent automatization, the PCA should contain explicit initial input components.

However, offering declarative input is *not* the same as frontal, teacher-centred learning. Explicit knowledge can be offered in several ways, including the potential utilization of accelerated learning techniques and rote-learning. Even regarding the explanation of grammar, Ranta and Lyster (2007) argue that there is no reason to limit this to deductive, metalinguistic instruction (such as the upfront presentation of grammar rules). Inductive tasks which encourage students to notice the gap between what they say and the corresponding target-language forms are likely to be more motivating; indeed, the declarative input stage allows for the use of a wide range of form-focused activities (see Chapter 4) as long as *by the end of it students have been presented with a combination of abstract rules and concrete examples*. The activities in this chapter are intended to give a taster of the many possibilities of how to achieve this.

2.1 Signs

Focus	Classroom language
Level	Beginners
Time	10-15 minutes
Preparation	Make a large copy of each sign and put them up on the classroom wall.

in class

1   To facilitate from the beginning the use of language useful for communication in the classroom put up the drawings on the walls and ask students to repeat the words for each several times.

2   Ask a few students come and point to one of the drawings for their classmates to say the words.

3   If possible, leave the drawings on the walls to remind them to use these expressions when they need to in order to use the language right from the beginning.

Can you repeat -
repeat -
repeat -
repeat...?

2.1 Signs

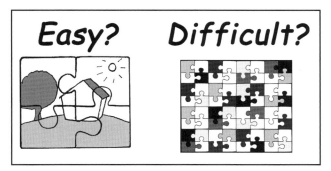

Easy? Difficult?

Can you s-p-e-l-l ?

LOUDER PLEASE

I have a question!

I don't know...

Acknowledgement

This idea comes from Carlos Pineda.

2.2 Thanks so much

Focus	Giving and receiving gifts
Level	Any
Time	20-30 minutes
Preparation	Write the phrases below on the board or Prepare a slide.

in class

1   Teach or review the language used to give and receive a gift. You can use the suggestions below, adding any others which might be useful for your students. Write them on the board or project from the computer. Make sure the students understand what each one means and ask them to repeat the phrases.

2   Ask students to work in pairs and tell them that they are going to give their partner a gift and they need to think of something their partner would really like. On a piece of paper they each draw a picture of the gift, being careful that their partner doesn't see it. When they finish, they fold the paper and they can draw a ribbon on it as if it were wrapped up like a gift.

3   When they have finished their "gifts", the Student As will give theirs to the Bs using some of the language learned and the Student Bs will make an appropriate response. The As may make a final response to close the conversation. Then the Bs do the giving.

4   With the whole class you can ask some students what their gift was.

GIVING	RECEIVING	RESPONDING
This is for you.	Thank you very much	You're (very) welcome.
Here's something for your birthday.	Thanks. I love it.	It's my pleasure.
I want to thank you for your help.	It's very kind of you.	I'm glad you like it.
I hope you like this.	It's lovely (great...).	
I saw this and thought of you.	It's just what I wanted.	

2.3

I am, it is

Focus	Adjectives with *-ed* and *-ing* endings
Level	Beginners to Lower intermediate
Time	20-30 minutes
Preparation	None

in class

1   Explain that in English some adjectives have two forms, one ending in *-ed* which can be used to describe how people feel and one ending in *-ing* which is generally used to describe a situation or a person that produces this feeling.

2   Teach them the examples below and be sure they are familiar with both the meaning and pronunciation of each. Point out the prepositions that the *-ed* adjectives are often used with.

3   Ask students to work in pairs and write two sentences, using one adjective of each type. They don't need to be the same – one sentence could be with *annoyed* and the other with *boring*, for example.

4   Go around the class and ask each pair to read their sentences.

bored (with)	boring
tired (of)	tiring
annoyed (at)	annoying
confused (by)	confusing
interested (in)	interesting
fascinated (by)	fascinating
embarrassed (about)	embarrassing
shocked (about)	shocking
frightened (by)	frightening
disappointed (by)	disappointing
amused (by)	amusing
excited (by)	exciting
surprised (at)	surprising
exhausted (by)	exhausting

Note

Students can easily confuse these words, so it's useful to provide plenty of practice so that they don't say things like "*Last night I watched television and I was very boring*".

2.4 Be a detective

Focus	Making deductions: modal verbs and phrases of probability
Level	Lower intermediate and above
Time	20-30 minutes
Preparation	Make a copy of the drawing below, large enough so all students can see it or make a one copy for each group of four students.

in class

1   Teach or review the vocabulary below which we use to make deductions.

2   Ask students to work in groups of four and show them the drawing of the bag. Tell them that they are detectives and that this bag was found by the police and that there is no identification in it. There was some money and they want to return it. So from the appearance of the bag they are going to try to make some deductions about who the owner is, using forms of the language studied, e.g. *It might belong to a woman...*

3   Give students a few minutes to prepare four sentences about the type of person they think the bag belongs to. Ask each group to read their deductions to the class.

It must/can't (be)	It could/might (be)	Surely/No doubt
Possibly/Probably	There's a good chance that	It seems likely that

Variation

Find on the internet a variety of scenes where something has happened previously (a house on fire, someone getting on an airplane, a child crying...), project these and ask students to choose one and write a short paragraph about what might have happened before the scene using the language studied.

2.5 Degrees

Focus	Expressing likes and dislikes
Level	Any
Time	15-30 minutes
Preparation	None

in class

1 Think of several things you like and say to your students: *I like..., I like swimming, I like going to the cinema, I like playing football.* Explain to them this is correct but that when communicating we usually try to use a variety of ways to say something to avoid repetition and to express more precisely what we want to say.

2 Teach or review the expressions below for liking and disliking, explaining that they refer to different degrees of the feelings, going more or less from weaker to stronger.

3 Ask students to think of a few things they like and dislike. Help with any vocabulary they may need.

4 Ask pairs and to talk about what they each like or dislike. Ask them to try to make this similar to a real conversation. Before they start also show them a few ways to agree and disagree with what someone has said previously or to express surprise/interest.

A possible conversation

A *I really like swimming.*
B *I don't much like swimming. Do you swim a lot?*
A *Every day.*
B *What I like to do is to go to the cinema.*
A *So do I. I'm crazy about horror films.*
B *I can't stand them but I love romantic films.*

2.5 Degrees

5   When students have had a few minutes to talk, ask them to change partners and start a new conversation about something else they like or dislike.

I rather like	I don't much like
I like	I don't like
I really like	I don't like… at all
I like…. so much	I dislike
I'm (really/so/very) fond of…	I (really) dislike
I love	I can't stand
I adore	I hate
I'm crazy about	I detest

Yes, I do too.	Oh, I don't.	Really?
Me too.	Not me.	That's interesting.
Yes, it's nice/fun….	That's not my sort of thing.	How interesting!
		Why?

This song and that song

Focus	Comparatives
Level	Elementary and above
Time	15-20 minutes
Preparation	Find two recordings of the same song.

<table>
<tr><td>in class</td><td>1</td><td>Review the comparative forms with your students. Include examples of the main forms they will need: as tall as, not as tall as, taller than, more expensive than, less interesting than... You could also mention some of the variations (happier than, good-better-best, bad-worse-worst).</td></tr>
</table>

2   Explain to your students you're about to play about 40 seconds of a famous song. (We have used John Lennon's *Imagine*, but see other suggestions below). Ask them to write down a word they would associate with the song (*nice, lyrical, moving*, etc.).

3   Now play the same song recorded by a different artist. Ideally, whichever song you choose, the second version should be quite different from the first.

4   Ask the students to write down the differences they notice. For example: *This version is faster than the first one. This version is not as moving as the first one. This version is as beautiful as the first one,* etc. You might want to provide students with some adjectives which can be used to talk about songs (see suggestions below).

5   When the song is over, encourage the students to share their notes with the person next to them.

6   Invite two or three of your students to share with the group. See if there's a consensus.

7   Alternatively, ask students to work in pairs and write a ten-line composition to highlight the differences, saying which recording they liked best and why.

> fast, slow, moving, sad, exciting, inspiring, melodic, calm, inspiring, rhythmic, discordant, harmonious, soft, loud, warm, dark, light, heavy, relaxing, happy, melancholy, powerful, resonant

Suggestions

Hey Jude (Beatles/Ella Fitzgerald)
Drive my car (Beatles/Bobby McFerrin)
I can't get no satisfaction (The Rolling Stones/John Scofield)
Imagine (John Lennon/Herbie Hancock Imagine Project).

2.7 Dear friend

Focus	Memorizing song lyrics
Level	Lower intermediate and above
Time	25-30 minutes
Preparation	Choose two short poems appropriate for the level and interests of your students. Make a copy for each pair of students.

in class

1 Show the first poem to your students. Give them time to read it and provide any help necessary. Review language for expressing reactions (see suggestions below).

2 Ask the students to work in pairs. The Student A's will dictate their impressions of the poem to the Student B's. Explain that you want them to dictate this as a letter, using appropriate letter salutation and closing, so they begin with *Dear friend...* and finish off with *See you soon*, or *Love*. The B's will write down what they hear without interfering, or asking questions. When the A's have finished dictating their 'letter', they sign it.

3 Next, the students read the second poem and change roles, so the B's dictate, and the A's write the letter.

4 Ask each pair to find another pair and exchange their letters with them. After reading the letters, students write a letter back to the author commenting on anything they agree or disagree with.

> **What I liked was... I didn't much like**...
> **The thing I liked best was... This reminds me of... I think that**...
> **In my view (opinion)... I was impressed by**...
> **I'm not sure I understood... I felt**....

Variation

The same exercise could be done using a song, or a picture, or a text. Also, instead of letters, the students may be asked to write a text message or a tweet.

2.8 Rote learning

Focus	Memorizing song lyrics
Level	Any
Time	20-25 minutes
Preparation	Choose a song that is interesting for your students, with words that are clear enough to hear. Write out the lyrics, leaving gaps for some words, and make a copy for each student.

in class

1   Choose a song that would be interesting for your students, of an appropriate level and in which the words are clear enough to hear. You can choose one that has several examples of a language point you would like to review (see below for some suggestions).

2   Hand out the lyrics, and ask students to fill in the missing words. Play the song so they can check that they have completed it correctly.

3   Depending on the length of the song and the number of students, divide the class into several groups and give each group one or two stanzas of the song to memorize. Give them five minutes or so to do this.

4   When all groups have memorized their part, play the song again and ask them to sing their part with the singer without looking at the lyrics.

5   Alternatively, without playing the song again after they have memorized their part, you can ask each group to say their part together, completing the whole song. For this, Cat Steven's *Father and Son* is useful as the song is a dialogue between two family members of different generations. Here you can divide the class in two groups and half the class speaks as the father and the other half as the son.

6   Ask students individually to write down five of the words that they memorized that they feel will be most useful for them and then compare with others in their group to see if they chose the same or different words.

Possible songs

Count on me (Bruno Mars) – First conditional
Hey Brother (Avicci) – First conditional, Interrogative sentences
Fernando (ABBA) – Past simple, Past continuous

Are you for or against it?

Focus	Speaking: Using discourse markers in presenting an argument
Level	Intermediate and above
Time	30-45 minutes, depending on the number of students in the class
Preparation	Prepare a slide of the table of discourse markers below or write them on the board.

in class

1 Explain the importance of discourse markers for constructing coherent discourse. Review the discourse markers below and add any others you might want to your students to work with. For the activity each discourse marker has a score next to it. You might want to vary these giving more points to those your students are least familiar with.

2 Present the subject the students are going to give an opinion about: celebrities' earnings, plastic surgery, ecology or whatever your students might be interested in talking about. Divide the class into two groups and give each group a position: Group A is for and Group B against. It doesn't matter if it has nothing to do with their real opinion, but they will have to think about an argument that defends that position.

3 Give the students one or two minutes to read the list again and write down their ideas.

4 Group A starts and each student presents one reason for their position, using as they do this as many discourse markers as they can. When they finish, each of the students in Group B presents a reason for their opposite position.

5 As the students speak, keep track on the blackboard of the points for each discourse marker they use to count them up at the end. Only give points if students use the discourse markers correctly. The group with most points will be the winner.

 Are you for or against it?

First of all (1)	However (1)
To start with (2)	At the same time (2)
As far as I'm concerned (3)	By the way (2)
From my point of view (1)	As a result (1)
To be honest (1)	Therefore (3)
What is more (4)	For this reason (2)
Moreover (3)	After all (2)

Variation

A member of Group A starts; then, a member of Group B continues and so on. That way, they can answer back to each other.

Acknowledgement

We learned of this activity from Angela Guerrero.

2.10

You can say that again!

Focus	Speaking: Agreeing, using intensifiers
Level	Lower intermediate
Time	15-20 minutes
Preparation	Make a copy of the list of adjectives for each student.

in class

1   Explain to the students that often in English two people express agreement by intensifying, e.g. A: *Beautiful day, isn't it?* B: *Glorious!* (Do a little work on the intonation here).

2   Hand out the list of adjectives below. Make sure the students know what they mean.

3   Now ask them to find the adjectives that go together (e.g. *good looking/gorgeous*).

4   Next give an example and ask the students to show agreement by using an adjective from the list that is stronger. '*We went out to the restaurant last night and we paid €100 each. That was expensive, I thought.*' *Expensive? Exorbitant!*.

5   Ask students to work in pairs and create mini-dialogues like the one above using all the adjectives from the list.

6   Students rehearse the dialogues, and then each pair says one of their mini-dialogues for the class.

Variation

Higher level students may also be invited to come up with their own adjectives.

nice	exorbitant
big	fascinating
expensive	beautiful
good-looking	huge
interesting	gorgeous
dirty	wonderful
tasty	delicious
pretty	filthy

2.11 Pessimists, optimists

Focus	Agreeing and disagreeing
Level	Intermediate and above
Time	20-30 minutes
Preparation	Prepare a list of sentences to read out in class.

in class

1 Start by telling the students whether you are more a pessimist or an optimist. Tell them what you feel optimistic about, and what you feel pessimistic about. See if this generates some reactions. You might ask for a show of hands to find out if they see themselves as optimistic or pessimistic.

2 Prepare a list of sentences to read to your students. It may be a few sentences from the coursebook with language you want your students to recycle or anything else that they can express an opinion about.

3 Review the language below for agreeing and disagreeing.

4 Ask the students to work in pairs. Explain that when you read out the sentence you would like the Student As to write a response beginning with '*Fortunately*', and the Student Bs will write a response beginning with '*Unfortunately*'. For example:

Read out: *I've heard Sarah and Tim are getting married.*

Student A might write: *Fortunately she's found someone who is just perfect for her.*

Student B might write: *Unfortunately, it won't last very long. She's too old for him.*

5 The students compare what they have written and then have a conversation where they can agree or disagree with what their partner has said.

6   Read out a few more sentences for them to carry out the same procedure.

> I really agree with you.
>
> I see your point.
>
> Yes, that is true.
>
> I know what you mean.
>
> You are right.
>
> That is a good idea.
>
> Yes, but we also need to consider....
>
> I don't think you understand the situation.
>
> I totally disagree.
>
> That can't be.
>
> I'm sorry but you are wrong about that.
>
> That's not the case at all.

CHAPTER 3
THE CONTROLLED PRACTICE PRINCIPLE

Introduction

While the overall purpose of language teaching is to prepare the learners for meaningful communication, skill learning theory suggests that – similar to the training of musicians or athletes – L2 instruction should also include *controlled practice activities* to promote the automatization of L2 skills. The purpose of this practice should be clearly explained to the learners and the content/format should be made as motivating as possible within the inherent constraints of the tasks. Admittedly, this latter goal is somewhat difficult to achieve – after all, repetitive drilling is not inherently engaging! – and therefore the natural inclination of most CLT practitioners has been to downplay the significance of such controlled practice. Unfortunately, however, without such repetitive rehearsal little effective automatization of L2 skills can occur. In this chapter, we would like to illustrate that it is possible to design 'communicative drills' that, although based on repetition, engage rather than demotivate the students.

As already discussed, the essence of controlled practice is to facilitate the students' move from relying on declarative rules to procedural knowledge by means of developing efficient procedures of automatizing the targeted L2 skills. This can take place through repetition within a narrow context, which is what drills are all about. Therefore, the key to the effectiveness of this stage is to design interesting drills that maintain the realness of meaningful communication. Several motivational strategies can be used for this purpose; for example:

- creating variation through modulating the speed, volume, or emotional content of how certain patterns or utterances are repeated;
- designing 'communicative drills' in which the content of the task is made psychologically authentic by means of personalization, intriguing through the activation of imagination and fantasy, or engaging through drawing on motives of youth or popular culture;
- combining communicative drills with role-play performance;
- disguising the drill in games, songs or chants;
- utilizing CALL programmes (i.e. language teaching software), which are often strong on creative and yet structured practice activities.

If practice is to be 'controlled', this should not only mean that we need to keep the context of the task narrow to ensure an inherently repetitive engagement with the activity in question, but also that the students' performance needs to be *monitored* and, if need be, corrected by appropriate *feedback*. Can this be done? Is this not a little bit like trying to square the circle? It is our experience that achieving a satisfactory trade-off is indeed possible, and DeKeyser and Criado (2013b) list a whole range of activity types – blank filling, matching, information and opinion gaps, controlled role plays, summarizing or finishing aural or written texts, jigsaw reading and listening – that can be drawn on to enrich controlled practice tasks in order to avoid the negative effects of mechanical drilling. We hope that the activities in this chapter will illustrate well how this principle can be borne out in practice.

3.1 Did you know…?

Focus	Asking and reacting to *Did you know…?* questions
Level	Lower intermediate and above
Time	20-30 minutes
Preparation	Make sure students have access to computers and the internet in class.

in class

1 Choose several topics you're fairly sure your students will be familiar with. (e.g., YouTube.com)

2 Ask students to work in pairs. Explain that, using the internet to find information, they each have to write five questions about one of the topics to ask their partner. Tell them all the questions begin with 'Did you know…?' For example, '*Did you know that the three founders of YouTube had worked for PayPal?*'

3 Allow the students some time to research the facts online, and write the questions. Circulate and make sure they don't all work on the same questions.

4 Students ask each other their questions.

5 When they've gone over the questions, ask them to think about what was said. Invite them to complete some of the following sentences:

I didn't know….
I was surprised to hear…
I can't believe…
I think it's amazing that…
I knew…

6 Finally, invite some of the students to read aloud some of their sentences and hold a plenary discussion.

Variation

If students don't have access to computers in class, they can prepare the questions for homework to ask the next day.

Not anymore!

Focus	Talking about past habits with *used to*
Level	Lower intermediate and above
Time	20-30 minutes
Preparation	None

in class

1   Ask the students to make a list of about ten things they used to do but they don't usually do anymore. (Examples: food they used to eat, games they used to play, things they used to say, clothes they used to wear, etc.). Give them some time to think and work on their list.

2   Ask students to work in pairs. Explain that Student As tell Student Bs their list this way '*I used to (play tennis twice a week) but now I (hardly ever/never play)*.', choosing *hardly ever* or *never* as is most appropriate. They should be talking for half a minute or so, while the Bs listen carefully without interrupting with questions or comments.

3   When the time is up, ask the Bs to report back to the As what they heard e.g. '*You said that you used (to play tennis twice a week) but that now you (hardly ever play)…*'.

4   Next ask them to change roles.

5   Hold a plenary discussion. Ask if they were all good reporters, or ask if someone said something humorous/strange/interesting, etc.

3.3

Ever so simple

Focus	Asking *'Do you ever ...?'* and *'Have you ever'...?*.
Level	Lower intermediate and above
Time	30-40 minutes
Preparation	None

in class

1   Write on the board:

    A)   Do you ever...?
    B)   Have you ever...?

2   Ask the students how they would complete the two stems above. If necessary, go over the rules again.

3   Then ask them to stand. Designate a *'Do you ever...?'* area and a *'Have you ever...?'* area in the classroom. Let the students decide which is which.

4   Explain that you'll read out the end of a question and that their task is to shout *Do you ever* or *Have you ever* and run to the corresponding area. So if the question is '*go to the cinema more than once a week*?' they need to shout *Do you ever* and then run to the *Do you ever* area. If the question is '*been to Japan*?' then they should shout *Have you ever* and run to the *Have you ever*... area. Keep it moving fast.

5   Now ask the students to sit down and write a few questions of their own. Call on a few students to read them out and the class responds as before.

Sample questions to read:

1.   ... **slept on a beach?**

2.   ... **forget telephone numbers?**

3.   ... **go to bed after midnight?**

4.   ... **met a famous person?**

5.   ... **speak to yourself?**

6.   ... **swum in a lake?**

7.   ... **climbed a mountain?**

8.   ... **go to the theatre?**

Variation

If you don't have room for students to run to the two areas, they could stand up and face the correct area when they shout out the answer.

3.4

We were saying...

Focus	Past continuous in reported speech
Level	Lower intermediate and above.
Time	20-30 minutes
Preparation	Prepare a slide of, or write on the board the sentences in step 1.

in class

1   Explain that the usual way to report something that was said using the present simple is to use a verb in the past simple: "I travel to London" becomes "She said she travelled to London every week". However if we are reporting several things in a conversation, we can use other expressions. Write on the board:

We were saying...
We were talking about...
I was telling (Jean/Marie)...
S/he was telling me...

Give them an example of a real conversation you had yesterday (or one you imagine):
I was talking with my neighbour and we were complaining about the weather. She was telling me that she didn't remember ever having so much rain this time of year.

2   Ask the students to stand up and walk around the room until you clap. When you clap, they get together with the person nearest them and begin a conversation on a given topic (the day so far, the week-end, their favourite hobbies, etc.).

3   Let them speak for a few minutes. When you clap again, explain that you want them to change partners and report their conversation using one (or more) of the phrases on the board.

4   Ask the students to change a few more times and repeat the procedure.

Note

This activity always generates a great buzz. Depending on the age of your students and the size of your group, you may need to be sure the noise level isn't too high.

Is there anybody who...?

Focus	Question forms
Level	Lower intermediate and above
Time	20-30 minutes
Preparation	Think of five attributes/skills/possessions/experience/etc. that students might have but which they are unlikely to know about each other (e.g. can bake a cake; has two dogs; has been sailing; sleeps on his/her stomach). Write them on the board.

in class

1   Tell students that their task is to find at least one person in the class of whom the target issues are true. In order to do so, they will need to go around and ask their classmates.

2   Discuss the appropriate question to ask for each issue and write them on the board.

3   Students then move around, asking each other the questions. They need to find only one person for each issue.

4   The winner is the student who first finds a classmate for each of the five categories.

3.6 I can chant

Focus	Fluency and rhythm
Level	Any
Time	15-20 minutes
Preparation	Prepare some examples of the target structure.

in class

1 Prepare sentences with the language to be practised. They should be somewhat rhythmical for the chant. For example, if you have presented the past simple, you might use the following:

What did you do last night, last night? What did you do last night?

2 Ask students to repeat together once or twice.

3 Then say the chant to one of your students and encourage them to answer something like this, also rhythmically:

Last night I went to the cinema, the cinema.
Then they chant the question again to the next person for them to answer.

4 If class size permits, go around the whole class. Otherwise, ask students to do the activity in groups of four or five.

5 After finishing, in a normal tone of voice you can ask the class what a few of their classmates did last night.

Variation

If you have been studying vocabulary for food, you might do this chant:
What do you want, what do you want, what do you want to eat?
I'd really like some soup (chicken, salad...), please, some soup please.

Note

Chants have been used effectively in many language teaching contexts. It is easy to invent sentences of this nature for any topic, and students practise the language in a way that is playful and more memorable than with a traditional drill. Gestures can also be added – for *last night*, you could point over your shoulder with your thumb to indicate the past, and for *what do you want to eat?* you could extend your open hand towards the other person as with an invitation.

3.7 Ha-ha-ha

Focus	Automatization of language; intonation
Level	Lower intermediate and above
Time	20-30 minutes
Preparation	Find one joke per student on the internet or from another source.

in class

1   For each student print one joke of the appropriate language level. If possible, each one should have some spoken language.

2   Give students their jokes and explain that they are going to tell their joke several times to different classmates so they will need to learn it, not read it. They don't need to tell it word for word and they may make little changes if they want. Emphasize that they should try to speak expressively when they tell it and vary the intonation.

3   When they have had a few minutes to learn their joke, ask them all to stand up and walk around the room. When you clap, they pair with the person next to them and each tells their joke. After they finish they each find another classmate and tell the joke again. They repeat this until they have told their joke at least five times.

4   When they have finished, ask for a few volunteers to tell one of the jokes they heard from a classmate.

Note

Gatbonton and Segalowitz (2005) stress the importance in language learning of creative automatization, which involves not memorizing rules but committing instances of language to memory. In this activity it is likely that segments of the jokes told repeatedly will stick in learners' memory.

Inner workbench pronunciation

Focus	Pronunciation
Level	Any
Time	5-10 minutes
Preparation	None

in class

1   Think of a specific word/sentence that your students need to practise pronouncing.

2   Tell them you are going to say the word/sentence once and then ask them to do something with it on their "inner workbench", in their mind.

3   Say the selected word/sentence clearly and then quietly ask students to hear it in their mind in your voice... Then in their voice... With many voices saying it together... Ask them then to whisper the word... And then to say it aloud.

4   Repeat whenever you find something that your students have difficulty pronouncing.

Note

Often simply repeating after the teacher over and over again doesn't lead to improvement as it is something done mechanically. This exercise leads learners to make a deeper connection with the language dealt with and thus to greater autonomy.

Acknowledgement

We learned this idea and the term "inner workbench", which refers to working with the inner processes of listening and speaking, from Adrian Underhill.

3.9 Creative drills

Focus	Using creative drills to automatize language
Level	Lower intermediate and above
Time	10-15 minutes
Preparation	None

in class

1 Divide the class into two groups.

2 Explain that the students in Group A each have to write sentences beginning with '*On the one hand...*'. Students in the Group B each write sentences beginning with '*On the other hand...*'

3 Ask them to write at least ten sentences.

4 When they've finished writing, have everyone stand, mingle, read their sentences to each other, and see if any sentences go with each other, using the construction *On the one hand... On the other hand*. If they find someone whose sentence goes with theirs, they stay at the front of the class together.

5 After a few minutes stop and have those who have matched their sentences read them to the class.

Variation

This exercise can be used to practise many other structures: for example, half the group writes sentences beginning: '*I was going to...*' ('*I was going to call you...*') and the other half writes: '*But ...*' (...'*but I worked late last night*'). Or also: '*I used to...*' '*but now...*'.

Note

In this activity students are repeating the language as with a drill but in a more creative and less mechanical way.

3.10 That is the question

Focus	Asking questions
Level	Lower intermediate and above
Time	40-50 minutes
Preparation	Make a copy of the *Find someone who...* grid for each student.

in class

1   Prepare a *Find someone who...* grid where students will need to use a structure you want to review, such as the present perfect in the example below.

2   Go over the formation and uses briefly.

3   Give each student a copy of the grid on the next page and explain that they will need to ask their classmates questions to find out who has done each of the things listed: *Have you sent an e-mail? Have you seen a film this week?...* When they find someone for each question, they write the name on the grid and the first person to complete the grid will be the winner.

4   After one student has finished, let the rest of the class continue for a few minutes.

5   Then ask the student who finished first, or different students if you prefer: Who has written a poem?, Who has seen a film this week? and so forth for all the items.

Variations

This can easily be adapted to work with other target structures. For example, past simple: *... came to class by bus, ... went to the theatre last weekend...* Or future: *... will go out with friends next weekend, ... will take a trip next month...* Or would like/prefer: *... would like to travel to England, ... would prefer to live in the country...*

Note

If you have access to a space outside the classroom, consider taking advantage of it to do the activity there, and if not, with a large group you might want to ask your students to work quietly.

3.10 That is the question

...has had a pet.	...has studied for an exam this week.	...has read a mystery novel.
...has spoken to a friend before class.	...has sent an email this week.	...has made a mistake recently.
has seen a film this week.	...has eaten in an Italian restaurant.	...has gone on a trip this year.
...has written a poem or a story.	...has been out of the country.	...has had a birthday this month.

3.11

Oh, by the way...

Focus	Breaking the ice: Using chunks
Level	Lower intermediate and above
Time	15-20 minutes
Preparation	Bring in one object for each group of four students (soft ball, dice, etc.).

in class

1   Ask the students to work in groups of four.

2   Give an object to each group.

3   Ask the group whether they know when '*by the way*' is used. Elicit examples, or an L1 equivalent.

4   Next have a ball in your hand, and say: *Hi, my name's Bruno and I like music. Oh, by the way, this is an orange.*

5   Now pass the ball to the student next to you, and invite him/her to say a similar example such as: *Hi, I'm Marie, and I like (going to the cinema). Oh and by the way, this is (an airplane)*, etc. Each student says something about himself/herself and invents something for the object to be.

6   Ask the students to work in groups of four. When all four have introduced themselves and practised the structure, take the object back from one of the groups and start again like this: *As I was saying, I like jazz and I play the guitar in a band.*

7   Now pass the object to the student next to you, and she says: *As I was saying, I like movies, I usually see two every week.* and so forth.

Note

We have used this exercise as an ice-breaker with groups meeting for the first time. Students give information about themselves and get to know each other a little, something very useful for a new group.

CHAPTER 4
THE FOCUS-ON-FORM PRINCIPLE

Introduction

As we have pointed out the PCA's emphasis on maintaining an overall meaning-oriented approach should not be at the expense of the formal/ structural aspects of the L2 that determine accuracy and appropriateness at the sentence, discourse and pragmatic levels. Therefore, an important feature of communicative language teaching in the 21ˢᵗ century will be finding the optimal balance between meaning-based and accuracy-based activities in the dynamic classroom context. Efforts to achieve this balance have been usually done under the banner of "focus on form" or "form-focused instruction", and the focus-on-form principle of the PCA represents the central thrust of these efforts.

Form-focused instruction explores the structural system of language from a communicative perspective. In many ways, it represent a halfway position between a concern for communicative meaning and the formal features of the language, calling for a primarily meaning-focused instruction in which some attention is paid to form. Thus, form-focused instruction can be seen as a new type of grammar teaching embedded within a communicative approach, and in that sense it is a prime example of trying to implement the explicit-implicit interface that we discussed earlier. One of the main proponents of the focus-on-form approach, Rod Ellis (2008), has drawn up the following comprehensive framework of the various form-focused options, distinguishing four macro-options:

1 *Input-based options* involve the manipulation of the language input that learners are exposed to or are required to process. The main types of this macro-option are *input flooding* (providing input that contains an artificially increased number of examples of the target structure), *enhanced input* (input in which the target feature is made salient to the learners in some way, e.g. by highlighting it visually in a text), and *structured input* (input that the learner is forced to process in order to be able to provide a required follow-up response).

2 *Explicit options* involve instruction that can be direct (learners are provided with metalinguistic descriptions of the target feature, e.g. in deductive instruction) or indirect (learners are provided with data illustrating the target feature and are required to 'discover' the rule for themselves, e.g. in inductive instruction).

3 *Production options* involve instruction geared at enabling and inducing learners to produce utterances containing the target structure. This type can be further subdivided in terms of whether it involves text-manipulation (e.g. fill-in-the-blank exercises) or text-creation.

4 *Corrective feedback options* involve either implicit feedback (e.g. recasts or clarification requests) or explicit correction (e.g. metalinguistic explanation or elicitation), and we can also distinguish between feedback that is input-providing (e.g. recasts or metalinguistic explanation) or output-prompting (e.g. requests for clarification or elicitation).

This framework shows that the *focus-on-form principle* is relevant to a wide range of applications. The activities in this chapter cannot cover all the possibilities but they are meant to offer a good illustration of how grammar and communication can be successfully matched.

4.1

It's all relative

Focus	Relative clauses
Level	Lower intermediate and above
Time	20-30 minutes
Preparation	Make one card for each two students with a word on it that your students will know.

in class

1   Present or review the basic information about relative clauses. You don't need to go into a great deal of depth but the main points should be clear for your students.

2   Ask students to work in pairs and give each pair a card. Tell them not to show the card to the rest of the class and to work quietly so the other students don't hear which word they have. They prepare together a definition of the word using a relative clause. For example, if the word is *computer,* they could say *"This is something which you use to send emails"* or *"This is something which has YouTube".*

3   Each pair reads their definition for the rest of the class to guess.

4   When all pairs have given their definition, have them try to remember as many as they can, writing the word with the definition: *A computer is something which you use to send e-mails.* Give them five minutes to write as many as they can and then ask each pair to say one other than their own until all the words have been defined again.

What has been done?

Focus	Passive
Level	Intermediate and above
Time	20-25 minutes
Preparation	Make copies or prepare slides of two 'spot the difference' pictures – where some details from picture 1 have been changed in picture 2.

in class

1   Review the formation and use of the passive voice in the different tenses.

2   Show the students Picture 1; if possible, project it from the computer. Ask one or two general questions about it and tell them to study it carefully for one or two minutes.

3   Take Picture 1 away and show them Picture 2 and have them write down as many sentences as possible using the passive voice to reflect the changes. *The scissors were put on the table/ the scissors have been moved. The trash was placed by the door* etc.

4   Ask the class for their ideas. See if they are able to mention all the changes. Accept answers in any tense that is appropriate.

Variation

When you do the activity, let students see both pictures at the same time to find the changes as memory is not a key element here.

Picture 1

Picture 2

4.3

The right way

Focus	Use of polite language
Level	Lower intermediate and above
Time	40-50 minutes
Preparation	None

Procedures

1   Explain to your students that sometimes even though a sentence is grammatically correct it is not the "right way" to communicate what you want to say. Give them an example such as this: When introduced to a very important person, someone says *"Tell me all about your project"* where a more appropriate alternative would be *"Could you please give me some information about your project?"*

2   Using examples such as those given below, show students some ways to make speech more polite.

> **Verb forms:**
>
> **Past – I wanted to ask....**
>
> **Past continuous – I was wondering if... , I was hoping...**
>
> **Modals – Could..., Would it be possible..., Would it be alright if....**
>
> **– It would be very helpful/I would really appreciate it if...**
>
> **– Would you mind... If I may say so...**
>
> **Softening words:**
>
> **– Please**
>
> **– For a moment**
>
> **– Just, only**
>
> **– Perhaps**

3   Write the sentences below on the board. Ask students to work in groups of three or four. Tell them that for each one they are going to write a sentence describing the context where it might be said and where a more polite alternative would be more appropriate. Then they will decide together on a more polite way to say it and write that under the context.

CHAPTER 4: THE FOCUS-ON-FORM PRINCIPLE

4 When they have had time to finish, collect the papers from each group and put them on the walls for the students to walk around the room and read those of other groups.

Help me with my report.

Let me use your pencil.

Give me the book

I want to see the doctor (dentist...)

Can I leave early today?

Note

To communicate not only do students need to learn how to understand language and to produce it, they also need to know how to use it appropriately. We know of the case of one student who was living with a host family abroad and whenever the mother would ask her "*Would you like to have dinner?*" she answered "*No*" and stayed in her room until she finally realized that she wasn't being asked a real question but being asked/invited to sit down and eat dinner with the family, even though it was at a different time from her home country.

Give me feedback

Focus	Writing: Asking for clarification and feedback
Level	Any
Time	10-15 minutes
Preparation	None

in class

1 Choose a language topic that you have presented to your students but they haven't worked with extensively. Think of a title for a short composition which would require them to use the language. (See examples below.)

2 Tell your students that they are going to write a composition on the title you assign. Give them about ten minutes to write it.

3 Before you collect the compositions to correct, ask your students to underline two or three things in what they have written that they have doubts about. Explain that it is these points that you will be correcting.

4 Correct only those points that the students have underlined. Try to return them as soon as possible. The corrections on what they have expressed doubts about are likely to lead to their being remembered better.

Past simple	*Last summer*
Present simple	*A normal day in my life*
Vocabulary for the house, furniture	*My house*
Vocabulary of personal qualities	*My best friend*
Conditional	*If I won the lottery…*

No one like you

Focus   Comparatives of equality
Level   Lower - intermediate and above
Time   25-30 minutes
Preparation Prepare slips of paper with the sentence below and the name of each of the students in the class. Distribute the strips so that each student has a slip with the name of a classmate on it

in class

1   Teach or review the structure *as...as* to express equality.

2   Ask two students who are the same height to stand up by each other and elicit from the class the sentence *A is as tall as B.*

3   Review positive adjectives to talk about people. Use the list below, adding any others examples you would like your students to know. After explaining the meaning of any they don't know, ask students to pronounce the words after you and then pronounce them silently and at the same time try to think of someone they know who has that quality.

4   Explain the structure *I'd like to be as _____ as _____.* Give an example or two. *I'd like to be as talented as* (name of someone you admire).

5   Give each student one of the slips of paper with the sentence and the name of one of their classmates. They think for a moment of a positive quality their classmate has – one of the ones studied or another – and write a comparative sentence on the paper. For example, *I'd like to be as <u>patient</u> as Hans.*

6   Students stand in a circle and one by one read their sentence and give the slip of paper to their classmate. If you don't have enough room for them to stand in a circle, they can stay in their desks and stand up when it is their turn to speak.

4.5 No one like you

clever	optimistic
nice	good-looking
fun	active
hard-working	elegant
orderly	patient
interesting	sensitive
brave	intelligent
generous	friendly
kind	wise
creative	studious
enthusiastic	talented
helpful	confident

I'd like to be as _____ as (name of student)

Note

It is best to do this activity after the students have been together long enough to get to know each other a little. It could be done the last day of the term to close the class in a way that will have students take a positive feeling about the class with them.

No one is perfect

Focus	Writing or Speaking: Error correction
Level	Any
Time	20-40 minutes, depending on the number of errors used
Preparation	Prepare a slide or make photocopies of a list of errors in learners' written production.

in class

1 For a period of time when checking written exercises, make a list of errors that appear repeatedly in different students' work.

2 Reassure your students that making errors in normal in the process of learning another language and that we learn from our errors as they tell us what we need to work on.

3 Ask students to work in groups of three or four and project the list of errors from the computer or have a photocopy for each group.

4 Ask them to read the sentences and try to find the errors and think of how to correct them. Provide them with some necessary language to discuss the errors (*This should be..., I think this is wrong...*).

5 When students have had the opportunity to work with the errors on their own, go over them, adding any information that might be needed for them to see how to correct the errors.

Variation

A similar process can be carried out with spoken production if students give oral presentations or do spontaneous role-plays.

Note

For learners to develop communicative competence they need to become both more fluent and more accurate. Sensitive error correction is important for them to develop greater accuracy.

4.7 In the cloud

Focus	Speaking: Past simple of irregular verbs
Level	Lower intermediate and above
Time	20-30 minutes
Preparation	Make photocopies or prepare a slide of a word cloud (see below).

in class

1 Prepare a word cloud (see www.wordle.net) using words for a topic you want to practise. In the example below, it would be the past simple of common irregular verbs. Review the verbs and the formation of affirmative, negative, interrogative, and short answers in the past simple. Project it from the computer or give each student a photocopy. Clarify the meaning of any verbs they don't know.

2 Ask students to find one verb in the cloud for something they did yesterday or last week and think of a sentence using it (e.g. *Last week I bought a new CD*).

3 Ask students to get up and walk around the room and at a signal from you (clap, ring a bell, stop the music you are playing...) they pair with the person next to them and Student A says their sentence "*Last week I bought a new CD*" and Student B says "*Yes, but did you...?*", adding another verb. For example, "*Yes, but did you go to the cinema?*" A will answer, *Yes, I did* or *No, I didn't*. Then they change and the Bs say their sentence and the As ask "*Yes, but did you...?*"

4 Tell students to think of another sentence referring to something they did and then repeat the procedure. Do this several times.

Special guest

Focus	Question formation in the present, past and future
Level	Lower intermediate and above
Time	30-40 minutes
Preparation	Choose a suitable story and make photocopies of it for each student. Ask a language assistant, a native speaker or someone whose level of English is considerably higher than that of your students to pretend to be an author and to come and talk to your class.

in class

1   Tell your students the story. Ask them to just listen.

2   Give them the transcript, allow time for questions they might have about the story.

3   Now announce to your class that you have a surprise for them: the author, the person who wrote the story, happens to be a friend of yours and has agreed to come and meet them.

4   Divide the class into four groups and give each a colour: explain to the Yellow group that you want them to write ten questions using the present simple. The Blue group write ten questions using the past simple. The Green group write ten questions using the present perfect. The Orange group write ten questions using the future.

5   Allow some time for this. Then ask the guest to come in.

6   The students take turns asking the questions.

7   When the guest leaves, ask the students to think about the guest's answers. Was there anything s/he said that surprised them? Anything that was curious? Funny? Really interesting?

Variation

The exercise can also be used with higher level students as well, but the task could be more challenging. For example, students might be asked to write ten questions using the third conditional.

My perfect future

Focus	Writing: Describing an ideal future life
Level	Lower intermediate
Time	30-40 minutes
Preparation	None

in class

1   Tell students to forget about today and to imagine their perfect future. Give suggestions, pausing for a moment between each so they have time to use their imagination: *In your perfect future where do you live?... What do you do every day?... What do you do for your holidays?... Who do you know?... See everything you can about your perfect future... .*

2   Ask one student what s/he thought of as the place to live. If the answer is "a big city", explain that after imagining their perfect life, to talk about what they imagined they wouldn't normally say *I live in a big city* but rather *I would live in a big city".*

3   Ask students to remember what they had imagined and then to write a composition on *What I would do in my ideal future.*

4   Give students time to write their compositions and then collect the compositions and put them on the walls for students to walk around and read. Tell students to try to find someone who coincides with them in some aspect. Alternatively, ask students to work in groups of five or six and read their compositions to each other.

5   Ask if anyone found something that was similar to what they wrote.

Note

In this activity students have a lot of exposure to ways of talking about the future, both in what they write and in reading what their classmates have written but in a context that is meaningful and interesting for them.

Get physical!

Focus	Revision of the past simple and past participle of irregular verbs
Level	Beginners to Intermediate
Time	10-15 minutes
Preparation	Write on the board or prepare a slide of a list of irregular verbs in their infinitive form.

in class

1   Take one of the verbs at random and demonstrate: Bend down, touch your feet (or as far down as you can reach) and say the verb (e.g. *take*). Then place your hands on your hips and say (*took*) Finally, raise your hands above your head and say (*taken*).

2   Ask the students to do the same with you.

3   Now call on students at random and ask them to choose another verb from the ones on the board. They first demonstrate the movements, and then the whole class does it.

4   Continue until you've done this for all the verbs.

5   Next, invite the students to think up of a verb not on the list they would like to demonstrate.

6   Ask a couple of students to demonstrate their verb and have the whole class do it with them.

7   Then explain that you want them to think of a multi-word chunk incorporating one of the verbs from the list on the board (i.e. *Take a shower, Go to sleep, Write a letter*). If the students can't think of one, they can ask you or a classmate for help. When everyone seems ready, ask several or all the students demonstrate their chunk, using the movements for the three forms.

Note

Harvard University neurobiologist John J. Ratey says "exercise improves learning on three levels: first, it optimizes your mind-set to improve alertness, attention and motivation; second, it prepares and encourages nerve cells to bind to one another, which is the cellular basis for logging in new information; and third, it spurs the development of new nerve cells from stem cells in the hippocampus" (Ratey 2008: 53). He adds that German researchers found that people learn words 20 percent faster when they are asked to perform some sort of physical exercise prior to the task. (p. 45).

Acknowledgement

We learned steps 1 and 2 from Mario Rinvolucri.

4.11 Input to intake

Focus Reading: Present simple and present continuous
Level Beginners to Lower intermediate
Time 10-15 minutes
Preparation Choose a suitable reading text and make a copy for each student.

in class

1 When working with a graded reader or a story that contains many examples of a structure you are currently presenting or reviewing with your students, give an explanation for the meaning and use of the structure, e.g. the difference between the *present simple* for for repeated actions or states and the *present continuous* for actions happening at the time of speaking.

2 Ask students to look at a part of what they will be reading and ask them to locate all the examples of the structures.

3 When they have had time to look for the examples, comment on a few with the students, showing them how they relate to the explanation given previously.

4 Invite them to try to notice more examples as they continue reading the text, either then or after class.

> It's early, but in the parks some people are taking their dogs for a walk. Or rather, the dogs are taking their owners for a walk. The dogs look happy and full of energy. Their owners look very tired. Other people are jogging and listening to their MP3s, doing some exercise before the working day begins.
>
> Buses are taking some early workers into the town centre. Street cleaners are picking up litter...
>
> Men and women are leaving for work....
>
> Some people are getting ready in the bathroom or they are waiting to use the bathroom. Sometimes their fifteen-year-old sister gets to the bathroom first and they have to wait for hours.
>
> Some people are eating breakfast... Some people are surfing the net or playing video games before they leave for school.
>
> (Hobbs, M. 2007 *David and the Great Detective,* Helbling Languages)

4.11 Input to intake

Variation

To work inductively, ask students to read the text first, look at the examples and try to work out the differences between the tenses if you haven't worked on this previously.

Note

This can be repeated with many other structures. You might look for texts with several examples of, imperatives, phrasal verbs, or order of adjectives to work with before they continue to read the whole text.

CHAPTER 5
THE FORMULAIC LANGUAGE PRINCIPLE

Introduction

'Formulaic language' is an umbrella term for a wide range of multi-word units such as expressions, idioms, lexical phrases, collocations or any conventionalized formulae (hence 'formulaic language'), that is, strings of words that hang together and form larger units in some way. Everybody knows that such lexical 'sums of the parts' play an important role in actual language use, but linguistics has only recently started to explore their significance in a systematic manner. This delay is rather curious, given that there is something fundamental about formulaic language. Henry Widdowson (1989: 135) was one of the first to argue that "communicative competence is not a matter of knowing rules ... It is much more a matter of knowing a stock of partially pre-assembled patterns, formulaic frameworks", and indeed many would agree with him that a communicatively competent speaker of a language is in command of thousands (if not tens of thousands) of language chunks of various length and coherence. These chunks are used as basic building blocks in producing both speech and writing, not unlike LEGO pieces used to construct an intricate structure.

In his famous 'idiom principle' John Sinclair (1991:112) has also underscored the important role idioms (his term for formulaic sequences) play in discourse. As he concluded, "The overwhelming nature of this evidence leads us to elevate the principle of idiom from being a rather minor feature, compared with grammar, to being at least as important as grammar in the explanation of how meaning arises in text".

Thus, Widdowson and Sinclair – two of the best-known applied linguists of the 20th century – were in full agreement that formulaic language competence is a basic ingredient of communicative L2 proficiency, and its significance can be compared only to that of grammar. The stakes get even higher when we realize that formulaic language competence is also directly linked to automatized, fluent language production (discussed earlier). Formulaic sequences are stored in the memory as *single units* and therefore their retrieval is cognitively relatively undemanding. This in turn allows the speaker to attend to other aspects of communication and to plan larger pieces of discourse, which would naturally facilitate fluent language production under real-time conditions. A great deal of everyday communication can be seen as assembling ready-made elements, which makes speech production as efficient as constructing a house from prefabricated units. Accordingly, promoting the mastery of formulaic language should be a featured component of the PCA; there should be sufficient awareness-raising of the significance and pervasiveness of formulaic language in real-life communication, and selected phrases should be practised and recycled intensively. The activities in this chapter demonstrate several ways in which this can be achieved.

5.1 Shouting chunks

Focus	Speaking: Learning lexical chunks
Level	Any
Time	5-10 minutes
Preparation	Write on the board, or prepare a slide of a list of lexical chunks.

in class

1   Read, or ask students to read, the list of lexical chunks aloud.

2   Ask the students to work in pairs.

3   Now ask them to each pick one chunk from the list on the board. Make sure they have chosen different chunks.

4   Next invite them to stand up. Explain that you want them to fake an argument and that they are only allowed to use their respective chunk. They're not allowed to change the word order, but they can change their voice (intonation, volume, etc.).

5   Let this run for a minute.

6   Finally, invite them to choose a different chunk. Explain that this time they have to pretend to make up after their argument and that they're only allowed to use their respective chunk.

Sample Language

You can say that again!

Good to see you.

Let's get out of here!

You must be joking!

You just don't seem to get it.

I'll see you later then.

S/he didn't have a clue.

That's ok with me.

Have a good one.

How's everything?

 **Shouting chunks**

Variations

1   After the activity, ask students to prepare short dialogues where they include four of the chucks and then present them to the class.
2   Prepare a written text with several gaps where learners need to put in a chunk that is appropriate. For example:

John: *Hi, it has been a long time.*

Michelle: _____

John: *I asked Heather where you were now but*
               _____

Michelle: *No, we never see each other. We are all so busy these days.*

John: _____. *It is really noisy here. Hard to hear anything.*

Michelle: _____

Stories we tell

Focus	Revising lexical chunks
Level	Intermediate and above
Time	25-30 minutes
Preparation	Make a copy for each student of the story, with the chunks removed. Write on the board or prepare a slide of a list of the chunks in random order.

in class

1   Explain to students that stories often use formulaic chunks.

2   Make sure the students understand the chunks in the list.

3   Explain to the students that you will read them a story and pause each time there is a lexical chunk for them to write down which one they think it is.

4   Tell the story, pausing for each underlined chunk. (See sample story and chunks below.)

5   When you have finished telling the story, read the version with the chunks included for students to check their answers.

6   Ask students to work in pairs to re-tell the story. Student A will begin and Student B will listen but explain that every 20 seconds or so, you will clap and then they need to change. The Bs carry on from where the As left off. Encourage them to use the chunks in the right places.

Variation

After reviewing the chunks, give students a copy of the text without the chunks for them to complete. Then tell them the story with the chunks included for them to check their work.

Comment

The chunks could be fairly typical of the storytelling genre, e.g., *once upon a time, one fine day,* and *guess what happened next?* or more general e.g. *for a very long time, I hear what you're telling me* etc.

5.2 Stories we tell

A Zen Story

Once upon a time, there was a young fellow who wanted to learn about a martial arts system. He thought about it very seriously, and one fine day, he decided to approach a well-known master and asked him earnestly: 'Master, I'm devoted to your arts, I'm a keen student, and I want nothing more than to become a master myself. How long do you think it's going to take me?' The master replied calmly: 'I hear what you're telling me. I reckon it'll take you ten years, or something like that'. As soon as he heard those words, the young man looked confused, was visibly angry, and snapped back: 'Ten years? Did you just say ten years? I can't believe this! But maybe you didn't hear me right, so let me say this again: I'm hard-working, I promise you, I've been wanting to do this for a long time, I'm prepared to devote my entire life to this, so how long, tell me, how long till I become a master like you?' The old master wasn't shaken, looked down, pulled his white beard, then he slowly lifted his chin, looked the young disciple in the eye and, guess what he said? He said: 'In that case, son, I reckon it will take you *twenty* years'

5.2 Stories we tell

A Zen Story

_____, there was a _____ who wanted to learn about a
_____. He thought about it very seriously, and _____, he
decided to approach a well-known master and asked him earnestly:
'Master, I'm devoted to your arts, I'm a _____, and
_____ than to become a master myself. How long
do you think it's going to take me?' The master replied calmly:
'_____. I reckon it'll take you ten years, or
_____'. As soon as he heard those words, the young
man looked confused, was visibly angry, and snapped back: 'Ten
years? Did you just say ten years? _____ But maybe you
didn't hear me right, so _____: I'm hard-working,
_____, I've been wanting to do this _____,
I'm prepared to devote _____ to this, so how long, tell me, how
long till I become a master like you?' The old master wasn't shaken,
looked down, pulled his white beard, then he slowly lifted his chin,
looked at the young disciple in the eye and, _____? He said:
'_____, son, I reckon it will take you _twenty_ years'.

I can't believe this

my entire life

one fine day

I hear what you're telling me.

Once upon a time

I promise you

In that case

young fellow

Let me say this again

keen student

Guess what he said?

I want nothing more

Martial arts system

Something like that

Numbers and chunks

Focus	Reflecting on lexical chunks
Level	Intermediate and above
Time	20-25 minutes
Preparation	Prepare photocopies or a slide or slips of paper, with about 25 formulaic chunks appropriate for the level and interests of your students. Give each one a number.

in class

1   Ask the students to choose a number from 1 to 25

2   Ask students to work in pairs, with someone who chose a different number.

3   Now show them the slide, and ask them to pick the chunk associated with the number they chose, or give them the appropriate slip of paper.

4   Leave the students some time to think about the following questions:

   • What does the chunk mean? (Help them with any doubts.)
   • When would you use it? (In a formal context? Informal?)
   • Do you use it actively? (If not, would you like to remember it?)
   • Does it have an equivalent in your language?

5   When they're ready, ask them to tell their chunk to their neighbour and talk about it. When the students have told each other about their chunks, ask them to pick another number and repeat the process.

Finishing the chunk

Focus	Listening and speaking: Using lexical chunks
Level	Lower intermediate and above
Time	25-30 minutes
Preparation	Find a suitable story to use.

in class

1 Write on the board (or dictate) a list of several chunks (see box below for some examples). Go over these with your students, make sure they know what they mean.

2 Explain that you will tell the students a short story, that from time to time you will insert one of these chunks randomly without any connection to the story but that you will only say the first word. The students' task is to supply the rest of the chunk. For example: *The story took place some twenty years ago **bread*** (students say: *and butter*). In this case make sure the students understand that the stress needs to be placed on *bread* and *butter* while the conjunction *and* is nearly imperceptible. In fact, in rapid speech, what is heard is *'n'* (as in rock 'n' roll, for instance). Work on this will help their spoken English and having to find the rest of the chunk can make it more memorable.

3 When the procedure is clear, start telling the story.

4 When you finish telling the story, ask the students to re-tell it in pairs. Student A tells the story, inserting randomly the first word of one of the chunks and Student B provides the rest of the chunk.

sick and tired	high and low
salt and pepper	far and between
to and fro	ups and downs
bed and breakfast	this, that, and the other
night and day	by and large
black and white	lock, stock and barrel
left, right and centre	ready, willing and able

Note

http://www.101zenstories.com is a good source of stories that are short and meaningful.

Rating chunks

Focus	Reviewing lexical chunks
Level	Lower intermediate and above
Time	10-15 minutes
Preparation	None

in class

1   Ask students to work in groups of three or four and have them go through their coursebook and pick six to eight lexical chunks.

2   Write the chunks up on the board and make sure the students are clear about their meaning.

3   Now explain to students that their task is to rate the chunks. Put the following questions on a slide or on the board:

1) Which do you think is hardest/easiest to learn?
2) Which is the most/least useful?
3) Which is the most/least colourful?
4) Which one sounds the most/least English?
5) Which do you like most/least and why?
6) Which is the strongest/weakest?
7) Which is the tallest/shortest?
8) Which is the richest/poorest?
9) Which is the fattest/slimmest?
10) Which is the prettiest/ugliest?
11) Which could be used as your group's motto? Why?

4   Ask students to discuss their answers in their groups and then have a whole class discussion to compare some of their answers.

Note

Questions 6-11 are intentionally 'funny'. We've found that mixing more 'serious' questions (such as 1-5 from the list above) with a few that may seem a little odd, allows the teacher to introduce a touch of humour, and to get students more interested in the task.

5.6 Categories

Focus	Recycling and categorizing lexical chunks
Level	Lower intermediate and above
Time	10-15 minutes
Preparation	Prepare a slide, or make photocopies, of the sets of chunks below.

in class

1 Write on the board: HAPPY – DIFFICULT – UPSET – EASY

2 Now hand out copies of the sets of chunks on the next page or show on a slide, helping with any they don't understand. Explain that these expressions are different ways to talk about the categories on the board and ask the learners to decide which of the above categories each set fits in.

3 Ask the students to check in pairs, then check with the whole class.

4 Finish by asking the students if they can think of equivalent chunks in their L1. Invite a few contributions from the class.

Variation

For more advanced students you could mix up the chunks and have them classify each one separately.

5.6 Categories

A	B
A piece of cake	A tough cookie
A walk in the park	(Be) in a pickle
An open book	(Be) in deep water
It's a cinch	(Be) in a real mess
There's nothing to it	A hard nut to crack
As ... as ABC	To bite off more than you can chew
Hands down	(Be) in dire straits
No sweat	It's no picnic
It's plain sailing	

C	D
(Be) on cloud nine	(Be) downbeat
(Be) tickled pink	Fly off the handle
A sight for sore eyes	Flip one's lid
(Be) over the moon	Have a fit
I 've never had it so good	Have a chip on one's shoulder
(Be) walking on air	(Be) down in the dumps
(Be) thrilled to bits	To get worked up
(Be) as pleased as punch	(Be) hot and bothered
	(Be) at the end of one's rope

5.7 Hold the phrase

Focus	Exploring language imaginatively
Level	Lower intermediate and above
Time	10-15 minutes
Preparation	Prepare a list of suitable phrases.

in class

1 Give the students some time to leave any worries or problems outside the classroom. Invite them to close their eyes or look down and pay attention to their breathing, observing how they breath in and out. You might wish to play some quiet background music to help them relax.

2 In this quiet atmosphere read a phrase (see sample below) at normal speed. Gently invite the students to feel the language, picture the words, hold the words near, and then slowly repeat them in their head, without uttering the words. Suggest they enjoy the sound of the phrase. Allow some time, and then invite the students to say the phrase back to you.

3 Do the same with several other phrases.

Sample Language

He's always making a scene

Could you say that again?

Put yourself in my shoes.

In the same way.

That kind of thing.

This sort of stuff.

And something like that.

Let me say this again.

It doesn't matter, in the end.

Speed it up

Focus	Memorizing lexical chunks
Level	Any
Time	10-15 minutes
Preparation	Write on the board or prepare a slide of a list of lexical chunks (see sample box below).

in class

1   Show the slide and read, or ask the students to read, the chunks aloud. This could be language the students have already seen and which they might need to recycle, or new input.

2   Go over the phrases one by one, make sure the meaning is clear and that the students know how to pronounce the phrases.

3   Ask the students to stand up and form a "train". Explain that you want the first student (the locomotive) to pick a chunk from the list on the board. Tell them this is going to be a fairly hilly ride.

4   When the locomotive picks up a chunk, everybody repeats it, non-stop. Now, explain that when you shout 'uphill' the train slows down and everyone repeats the chunk more slowly like this 'I... don't... know... what... you... mean'. When you say, 'downhill' the train picks up speed and everyone repeats the chunk faster.

5   Give several other students the opportunity to be the locomotive and pick another chunk. When the locomotive has chosen a new chunk, he or she can also be the one to shout *uphill* and *downhill*.

Have a good time!	**I don't know what you mean.**
(I'll) Catch you later.	**You win some, you lose some.**
(Do you) know what I'm saying?	**At the end of the day.**
Long time no see.	**To cut a long story short.**
It doesn't make any sense.	**That's the way you do it.**
What about you?	**Most of the time.**

Note

Neurobiologists tell us that when we're learning a new word, the first time we hear it, the nerve cells tasked for a new circuit fire a signal between each other. If we never practise that word again, the attraction between the synapses dies out, the signal is weakened and the word is simply gone. There is evidence that repeated activation, or practice of a given item causes the synapses to swell and make stronger connections, which is what exercises of this type try to achieve.

Chunking on the walls

Focus   Writing: Putting lexical chunks in context

Level   Intermediate and above

Time   30-40 minutes

Preparation   Write several lexical chunk on different sheets of paper, (see suggestions below).

in class

1   Put the sheets on the walls of the classroom or on desks in different parts of the room. Make sure the students understand all the chunks.

2   Ask students to work in groups of three or four. Each group stands by one of the papers and together decide on a context to write for the chunk. For example, with *"...thinks nothing of..."* they could write: "*My neighbour thinks nothing of playing loud music late at night*". At a signal from you, each group moves to another paper, reads what the previous group wrote and adds a different possibility.

3   Repeat this until the groups have had the opportunity to write a context for most or all of the lexical chunks.

4   Take the papers off the walls or the desks and tell students you are going to read each list of sentences twice. They should decide which sentence they like best and when you read them the second time they vote individually on their favourite.

... learned their lesson...

Needless to say...

It sounds like...

To cut a long story short...

... thinks nothing of...

... take care of...

... by heart...

... for a number of reasons...

All in all....

I have to say....

... a great way to...

Families of chunks

Focus	Speaking: Using lexical chunks in in real-life situations
Level	Lower intermediate and above
Time	30-40 minutes
Preparation	Write on the board or prepare a slide of a list of lexical chunks related to a communicative situation

in class

1   Choose an area of a specific linguistic function and select several lexical chunks related to that "family".

2   Read, or ask students to read the chunks aloud and make sure they understand them all.

3   Ask students to work in pairs and create a role play where, in the example given, one is the shopper and one the shop assistant. They should include several, though not all of the chunks.

4   Each pair performs their role play, stopping when a chunk comes in the dialogue. The rest of the class supplies the relevant chunk. If the class is large, call on three or four pairs or, alternatively, have each pair perform their role play for one other pair.

5.10 Families of chunks

Shopping

May I help you?

...pay with a credit card

... try it on

...just looking (browsing)

How much.....

Anything else?

That should be it

Keep your receipt

...get a refund

On sale

fitting (changing) rooms

That's a rip-off

window shopping

top brand

out of stock

How about...?

made of

get a discount

wrap it up

Note

Another day this can repeated with a different "family" related to other useful communicative situations (e.g. eating in a restaurant, asking for directions, apologizing and accepting apologies...).

A pair of chunks

Focus	Matching lexical chunks
Level	Intermediate and above
Time	5-10 minutes one class and 10-15 minutes the next class
Preparation	Print out strips of paper with the paired lexical chunks below. There should be one strip with two parts for each two students. If you need more, you can repeat a few.

in class

1   At the end of one class review the lexical chunks on the chart below to make sure your students know the meanings. Don't give the whole sentence and don't review them in relation to the other part. Use impersonal forms (*get something off one's chest, give someone a lift,* etc.).

2   For the next class cut the strips of paired chunks in half and hand them out randomly. If you have more students, you can give some the same strips, or you can create more pairs.

3   Ask the students with the second part (beginning ---) to stand on one side of the room and the other students walk over to them and say their part until they find someone who has the second part. They should then stand together. Check they have the correct parts.

4   When all students have found their partner, each pair will read their little dialogue for the rest of the class. Suggest they try to make their conversations sound as natural and realistic as possible.

5.11 A pair of chunks

I'd like to have a **night out on the town.**	---That **suits me** fine.
Why don't you **give me the lowdown**?	---Thanks. I need to **get it off my chest.**
I'll **get back at** you for this.	---**Calm down**.
Oh dear. My car is **as dead as a doornail**.	---Can I **give you a lift**?
Something fishy is going on.	---**You'd better believe it**. It's very strange.
I thought they'd **had a row**.	---No, he has just **popped the question**.
She **put her hopes** on him.	---And he **let her down** again.
I don't have any idea where I put your book.	---**Never mind**. I'll find it.
She was really **looking forward to** the trip.	---She **made a reservation** months ago.
You haven't **made a decision** yet?	---No, I'm still **turning things over in my mind**.
You aren't going to **rock the boat**, are you?	---No, I **wouldn't dream of it**.
I'm **worried sick** about starting my new job.	---Don't worry. You'll **learn the ropes** quickly.

CHAPTER 6
THE LANGUAGE EXPOSURE
PRINCIPLE

Introduction

According to the *language exposure principle*, the PCA should offer learners extensive exposure to large amounts of L2 input that can feed their implicit learning mechanisms. Why is this necessary? After all, as we said before, the difficulty of L2 learning is exactly the fact that the implicit learning processes that power L1 acquisition in children does not seem to work efficiently later. While this is true, in spite of its limitations, implicit learning still plays an important role in mastering a second language. We have already talked about the process of 'proceduralization' whereby explicit knowledge is transformed into implicit knowledge that in turn fuels fluency, but fluent speech is not the only area where implicit knowledge is relevant. To offer but one illustration, let us consider advanced language learners: part of their L2 competence involves a clear sense of what is common or, more interestingly, what is rare or unusual in the target language. This intuitive knowledge is very helpful because it helps them to choose language forms that are appropriate in a given situation. The question is, where does this knowledge come from? The only way learners can develop this intuitive sense is through implicitly registering somehow in their memory (by creating memory traces) *all* the language input they encounter when exposed to the L2. This is analogous to the well-known phenomenon that whenever we see a short extract of a film, we can usually tell straight away whether we have seen the film before or not; this can only happen if we have implicitly stored memory traces of all the films we have seen in our brain, which then scans this database to decide whether the new film extract matches any stored memories. Language exposure generates similar implicit L2 memory traces, which then help learners to operate in the L2 more competently.

Because implicit learning is by definition without conscious attention, learners are not aware of how the storing of these memory traces actually happens. The acquired implicit knowledge is the outcome of a mental language processing unit, and in order to keep this processor going, a large amount of L2 input is needed. The exposure necessary for this input can be achieved in several ways, most notably through extensive reading and listening tasks, watching films and television programmes in the L2 and of course interacting with L2 speakers (the latter will be discussed in the next chapter). Significantly, we can augment the implicit learning processes that take place during these tasks by applying some explicit scaffolding, thereby achieving effective implicit-explicit cooperation. Such scaffolding might include explicit task preparation through activities such as pre-reading/listening/watching tasks or initial explanations of certain aspects of the material. These will prime the students for maximum intake.

6.1 Getting ready for reading

Focus Reading: Understanding the main ideas

Level Lower intermediate and above

Time 5-10 minutes

Preparation Choose a reading text accompanied by photos or illustrations, with a title, and subtitle. You can use a text from your coursebook or photocopy a text from another source.

in class

1 When you are going to introduce your learners to a reading text, whether in the coursebook or one you have selected for them, ask them to look first at the title and any subtitles and photos.

2 Ask them a few general questions to see what they know about the topic. If there are words in the title or subtitles they don't know try to lead them to guess what they mean.

3 See if they can make any predictions about what they might find in the text. Then have them look quickly at the first one or two paragraphs to get the main ideas. To encourage them to get used to reading quickly and not stopping to decode each individual word, tell them they will only have two or three minutes.

4 Check to see if they found the main ideas and then ask them to predict what they think they will find in the next paragraph, and now give them a little less time to read it and then check if their predictions were correct.

5 When they finish, point out to them that while they may not have understood everything in the text, they were able to process quite a lot in a very short time.

6 Invite them to continue reading the rest of the text in this manner, in class or at home, before reading in a more detailed manner to complete any activities associated with the text.

Note

Working with a text in this manner can help learners to develop skills for reading longer texts more quickly, with greater fluency.

6.2 In the shadow

Focus	Listening comprehension and pronunciation
Level	Lower intermediate and above
Time	10-15 minutes
Preparation	Choose a listening text that your students have heard before.

in class

1   Tell your students that they are going to listen to something they have heard before and that they won't have to answer any questions on it. All they need to do is listen. Play the text.

2   Explain to students that they will listen again but this time they are going to shadow the speakers, i.e. to listen to a short bit and then repeat it to themselves as closely as possible to what they have heard. Then they will return to the text and listen for a moment and then find another bit to shadow. Continue this for a few minutes.

3   In pairs they comment on the experience and tell each other any bits they remember shadowing.

4   Point out to them that this can be a very useful technique for improving language skills such as listening and pronunciation.

Extension

Assign students to do extra listening outside class during the week and to keep a record of what they do (see below). They can listen to course book CDs if they have these, to radio/TV programmes in English or to many things available on the internet. You might give them some suggestions for interesting links which would be appropriate for their level and interests but it is often good to let them find their own. Check the records they keep the following week.

6.2 In the shadow

---

1. What texts did I shadow?

2. What did I learn?

3. How do I feel when I shadow?

Acknowledgement

We learned about shadowing from Tim Murphey.

Sharing

Focus	Reading: Choosing authentic texts
Level	Any
Time	5-10 minutes in class, plus homework
Preparation	None

in class

1   If you are teaching in a context where English is a foreign language and thus not everywhere around your students, brainstorm with them where they might be able to find texts written in English outside the classroom. Some options would be newspapers, the internet, tourist brochures, readers, instructions on how to play a game, etc.

2   Explain to your students that reading is a very important way to have contact with the language outside the classroom, especially if they are in a foreign language context. For this reason, you want them to do a lot of reading but you also want them to have texts that they will enjoy reading so they are going to find texts that they like. During the next week they will each locate a text they feel would be interesting for the class and either print it if it is on the internet or make a photocopy. Ask them to write a title for the text on the top of the paper. Texts for beginners will need to be easy and may be fairly short but encourage students at higher levels to look for texts - or parts of a larger text - of at least one or two pages. One example could be two or three pages from a graded reader appropriate for their level. Bring a few texts yourself that you think might interest your students.

3   Make a list of the titles, leaving space in two more columns after teach title. Put the collection of texts in a box and invite students to select one before or after class at some time during the week and to write their name on the list by the title in the second column. Give them a few days to read it and when they finish, they should write a short comment on the list by the title and their name in the third column and then choose another text, again writing their name. When they choose a new title they can read the comments written by their classmates.

4   If you continue the activity for several weeks, you could use the list to ask students who have read the same text to work in pairs or groups of three to talk about the text briefly.

Note

To protect the texts you could put each one in a plastic envelope.

6.4 Log in

Focus	Reading: Keeping a log of extra reading texts
Level	Lower intermediate and above
Time	10-15 minutes in class
Preparation	Make a copy of a reading log for each student (see example below).

in class

1 Discuss the importance of reading and ask students what they read in their own language during a normal week.

2 Ask students to work in pairs and tell each other if they like to read, when they read and what is something interesting they have read.

3 To encourage reading, tell learners they are going to keep a reading log. At least once a week, but more often if they want, they are going to read something in English which hasn't been assigned as part of the classwork. Suggest things such as an optional graded reader, something they want to know about on internet, even the ingredients in English listed on the package of a food product.

4 Give each student a log for them to keep in their notebook – see a possible template below. Decide on how often they should include an entry.

5 Collect the students' logs occasionally and make a comment for each student to encourage them to read.

6.4 Log in

MY LOG	Name
Date	What I read

Walking the walls

Focus	Reading: Scanning for specific information
Level	Any depending on the texts chosen
Time	40-50 minutes
Preparation	Make copies of several texts to put on the wall. Prepare two photocopies for each student with questions about the texts (see steps 2 and 3).

in class

1   Find several texts, such as pages from a graded reader or a newspaper or magazine articles, of a suitable level for your students. Six to eight is a good number. If the whole text is too long to read quickly in a few minutes, use only a part of it. Put the texts on the walls around the classroom.

2   Ask students to work individually. Give each student a paper with a question on each text which can be answered by scanning the text very quickly. Ask them to "walk the walls" and look for the answers to the questions. They can start anywhere so there won't be too many people at one text at the same time.

3   When they have finished, give them a second paper with a question on each text which they will need to read more carefully to be able to answer and have them "walk the walls" again.

4   Tell students to look at the texts once more until they find something they thought was particularly interesting and to write it down.

5   With the whole class correct the answers to the questions on the two papers and ask several students what they found interesting.

Note

If you have a large number of students in the class, you might consider using fewer texts and putting up two copies of each on opposite sides of the classroom for students to have easier access to the texts.

Mind the gaps

Focus	Listening: Noticing examples of interesting language
Level	Intermediate and above
Time	20-30 minutes.
Preparation	Ask a language assistant, a native English speaker, or someone whose level of English should be considerably higher than your students) to come and talk to your students.

in class

1   Tell students that you've invited a guest to come and talk to them. Ask the students to draw three columns on a piece of paper: In Column A they should note examples of language they find interesting. In Column B they should note examples of language they are familiar with but which they normally don't use themselves. In Column C they should write examples of language that's unfamiliar.

2   Invite your guest to come into the classroom. He or she might wish to tell your students a story, or talk about his or her country, or about a favourite hobby. This should last for about 10 minutes.

3   After the guest leaves, invite the students to share their lists with someone next to them.

4   Collect their lists and go over what they've written, clarifying doubts and providing explanations for any problems you see.

I'll tell you

Focus	Reading and speaking: Retelling a story
Level	Lower intermediate and above
Time	5-10 minutes in one class and 20-25 minutes in another class.
Preparation	Choose a suitable story to tell your students and find some links on the internet for stories they would be able to understand; the stories should be fairly long for their level.

in class

1   Say to your students you are going to tell them a story but you won't ask them questions on it. You want them simply to enjoy the story. Tell the story.

2   Give them links to stories in English on the internet and ask them to look at them and select one to prepare to tell in class. Ask them to bring you the name of the story and then give them a few days to read it, work with the text to be sure they understand it and prepare notes to help them to tell it in class.

3   The day they are going to tell the story ask students to work in groups of three or four, checking the titles to make sure that in each group no one has the same story. Inform them that they will need to retell one of the stories they hear.

4   In turns, they tell their story to the other students.

5   When they all have finished, ask them to work with someone from another group and tell briefly what one of the other stories they heard was about.

Possible sources for stories

http://www.awesomestories.com/
https://www.teachingenglish.org.uk/britlit
Besides the internet, they could also look for stories in English from books in a library.

Listening challenges

Focus   Listening for specific words and structures

Level   Lower intermediate and above

Time   15-25 minutes (depending on the length of the listening material)

Preparation   Choose a recorded dialogue and select six words in the dialogue for students to listen out for.

in class

1   Write the six words you chose from the dialogue on the blackboard in alphabetical order. The students must decide on their order of appearance in the dialogue. A word occurring several times makes the exercise more difficult. Play the dialogue for them to check.

2   As they listen a second time ask students to write down the words they hear after the six words. (If it is possible, choose words from phrases, and then the students' task is to provide the complete phrase.)

3   While listening to the dialogue a third time, students are to count certain words. For example: How many times do they hear articles? How many different prepositions? How many passive constructions? How many proper names? etc. The word type will depend on the dialogue and the instructional focus area.

Note

The aim is to give the students exposure to the language in the dialogue several times while they are busy doing easy problem-solving exercises.

6.9 I hear you

Focus	Active listening
Level	Lower intermediate and above
Time	20-25 minutes
Preparation	The day before doing this activity ask students to prepare a two or three minute talk about something that interests them for homework.

in class

1   Remind your students about the importance of the listener in a communicative situation. Go over with them different short expressions we often use to show the speaker that we understand or that we need more explanation (see below).

2   Also point out how we often use our body language to show we are listening and interested in what someone is saying.

3   Ask students to work in pairs. While Student A talks, Student B listens actively, using appropriate body language and some of the expressions studied.

4   When both students have given their talks, they find another pair and each person tells the others something they learned from their partner.

Yes, very true.	**Sorry, I don't understand what you mean.**
I see.	
Uh, huh.	**Could you explain that please?**
I agree.	**Excuse me, what was that?**
Good.	
I understand.	
Yes, I know what you mean.	
Interesting.	

CHAPTER 7
THE FOCUSED INTERACTION PRINCIPLE

Introduction

The final PCA maxim, the *focused interaction principle*, posits that the development of L2 communication skills requires ample opportunities for the learner to participate in genuine L2 interaction. The rationale for this principle can be presented on at least three different levels:

- First, we have seen that that participatory experience in real-life-like situations has been a fundamental aspect for communicative language teaching right from the beginning. Communication skills can only be fine-tuned by engaging in actual communication, and although we argued that this principle did not provide CLT with sufficiently precise guidelines, it remains an important aspect of the method if complemented by additional directives (such as the other six PCA principles).
- Second, there is a considerable body of research in SLA which indicates that "learners can benefit from taking part in interaction because of a variety of developmentally helpful opportunities, conditions, and processes which interaction can expose them to. These include input, negotiation, output, feedback, and attention" (Mackey and Goo, 2013: 1). In other words, interaction is an indispensable learning channel for several specific aspects of SLA.
- Third, participation in communicative situations can also be seen as the final stage of skill learning theory – *open-ended practice* – discussed earlier. This stage involves the continuous improvement in the performance of a skill in a less structured way than the previous controlled practice stage. In many ways, this stage 'seals' the progress and is comparable to a novice driver's experience of driving in real traffic after he/she has passed the driving test.

Thus, there is solid support for the claim of the focused interaction principle that newly acquired communicative skills need to be put into practice to become fully automatized and transferrable across a range of situations. Some of the best ways of achieving this involve study abroad experiences, which can dramatically improve the learners' communicative competence (cf. e.g. Collentine, 2009). In addition, including some kind of explicit focus to the experience of engaging in L2 interaction can augment the implicit learning processes in the same way as adding pre-task activities to listening or reading tasks discussed in the previous chapter. Such explicit focus might take the form of highlighting specific formal or functional elements to pay attention to, or encouraging learners to try and incorporate specific L2 phrases in their speech. The usefulness of such explicit scaffolding has been evidenced even at the level of study abroad programmes. In a project developed by Celia Roberts and her colleagues (2001), study-abroad students received advance training to complete an ethnographic study of an individually chosen aspect of the host country, and this explicit focus was found to make the period abroad a significantly more active and rewarding – learning experience for most of the participants. Similarly Paige et al. (2002) have compiled a collection of relevant materials, strategies and techniques titled *Maximizing Study Abroad: A Students' Guide to Strategies for Language and Culture Learning and Use.*

7.1 My advice

Focus	Giving and receiving advice
Level	Intermediate and above
Time	20-25 minutes
Preparation	Write on the board or prepare a slide of a list of useful phrases for giving and receiving advice (see suggestions below).

in class

1 Review useful language for giving and receiving advice. Make sure students know how to construct the complete sentence (e.g. *You might try* needs a verb + *-ing*).

2 Ask students to work in pairs and explain that Student A is going to tell Student B about a problem and B will give some advice using the language studied and a few other comments. A will respond. Then they change roles.

3 Students can ask for advice about a real problem they have but in case they don't want to talk about anything personal, you can write a list of problems on the board for them to choose from (see suggestions below).

I would advise you to…	Yes, that is very helpful.
My advice is to…	That is a good idea.
If I were you, I would…	Why didn't I think of that?
I think it would be a good idea to…	I could try what you suggest.
You might try…	I'm not sure if that would work.
Why don't you…?	Yes, I hadn't thought of that.
One option would be to…	

7.1 My advice

Possible problems

You are afraid you are going to fail an important class.

You want to buy a present for a friend but you don't have enough money.

You saw a friend shoplift something in a store.

Your best friend is gossiping about you.

7.2 Be a critic

Focus	Expressing opinions about a song
Level	Lower intermediate and above
Time	20-25 minutes
Preparation	Choose a suitable song and make a photocopy of the lyrics for each student.

in class

1   If you have access to the internet in your classroom, show your students a few album reviews (www.rollingstone.com is a good place to start). Go over difficult language when necessary.

2   Now ask students how they would define a 'good' song, with particular emphasis on the lyrics.

3   Give your students the sample language below, explaining expressions they might not know and adding any others you think would be useful to talk about the song you have chosen to play. Explain that they'll listen to a song and that you want them to prepare a critique of the lyrics using the language from the box and anything else they feel would be appropriate.

4   Hand out the lyrics and play the song.

5   Ask students to prepare their critiques. Give them a few examples: Line 1: *Great use of metaphor*. Line 4: *This is pretty hollow*.

6   When they've finished, students work in pairs and talk about the song and see if they have the same opinions.

7   Hold a plenary discussion.

Great use of metaphor!	**Intense.**
This is pretty hollow.	**It really says a lot to me.**
Too romantic/syrupy.	**That is exactly how I feel.**
Haunting.	**It's a bit dated.**
This doesn't make any sense.	**Good vibes**
Very profound.	**Intriguing**
This is vivid.	**It relaxes me a lot.**
So exciting!	**Very invigorating**
What a tear-jerker!	**It stirs my imagination.**
This really lifts my spirits.	**Makes me feel depressed.**

7.3

Ring, ring

Focus	Speaking: Making telephone calls
Level	Intermediate and above
Time	15-20 minutes preparation and 2-3 minutes per pair
Preparation	Make a copy of the functions related to phone calls for each pair; Make copies of the role-play cards.

in class

1   Ask the students to work in pairs and give them a copy of the following functions related to telephone calls. Ask them to write down words and phrases connected with each function. After a few minutes, ask pairs to share their ideas with the rest of the class.

- **Making contact**

- **Giving more information:**

- **Taking a call**

- **Asking for a name / information**

- **Asking the caller to wait**

- **Telephone problems**

- **Leaving / Taking a message**

7.3 Ring, ring

2   Put two chairs back to back and explain to the class that each pair will come up and sit in the chairs to perform improvised role-plays. As those role-plays will be for speaking on the telephone, they will not be able to see each other. Give each pair one of these situations or others suitable for your students and let them have a few minutes to organize what they want to say. Then call on each pair to present their role-play for the rest of the class.

Acknowledgement

We learned about this activity from Jasmina Niezgoda

A: You promised your mother that you would water her plants while she was away on vacation.
You forgot. The plants are dead. The phone rings.

B: You are away on vacation in San Francisco. You have a lot of beautiful plants. Call your son/daughter to find out how your plants are doing.

A: It is Saturday evening. You are very bored so you call your friend to see if he/she would like to go out this evening.

B: You have a lot of work to do before Monday. You don't know if you can finish your project but you are tired of working. The phone rings.

A: You call your friend's house but someone you don't know answers. You ask is your friend is there.

B: You are staying with your friend. You have just gotten up and haven't seen your friend yet.
The phone rings.

7.3 Ring, ring

A: You are calling your friend Ken. You want to invite him to a party this Friday.

B: You answer the phone. The person on the other end of the line wants to speak to Ken.
You don't know anyone named Ken.

A: You need to get in touch with someone urgently because you need their help to finish a project. You call to ask about this.

B: Someone calls the office where you work to speak with a colleague who has left the office for an hour.

A: You want to reserve a table for five at a restaurant called the Slanted Door. Call the restaurant and make a reservation for 8:00 pm this Saturday.

B: You work at a restaurant called the Slanted Door. Answer the phone. (The restaurant is completely booked for Friday and Saturday nights this week.)

A: You need to make a doctor's appointment because you hurt your back while you were cleaning the house. Call the doctor's office and make the appointment

B: You work in a paediatrician's office answering the phone. (Note: a paediatrician is a doctor for children.)

A: Your friend just borrowed your car to go get some more beer. Call him (on his cell phone) to remind him to get some chips.

B: You borrowed your friend's car to buy more beer. You have just driven into a lamppost. You're not hurt, but the car is badly damaged. Your cell phone rings.

7.3 Ring, ring

> **A:** You're on vacation with your friend in Las Vegas. You have just spent all your money. Your friend is upstairs in the hotel room. Call your friend and ask to borrow $60.
>
> **B:** You're asleep in your Las Vegas hotel room. Your friend is still downstairs in the casino.
> It's four o'clock in the morning. The phone rings.

> **A:** You haven't finished writing your English essay. Call your teacher in his/her office and ask if you can turn it in late.
>
> **B:** You are a rather strict English teacher. Unless there is a very good excuse, you always follow your rules.

Talk, talk, talk

Focus	Speaking: Conversational language
Level	Lower - intermediate and above
Time	20-30 minutes
Preparation	Make a copy of the list below for each student.

in class

1   Give students their copy of the list and explain that when we have conversations we do different things such as these. Provide them with expressions they might need for some of them (Ask for clarification: *Could you explain that please?* Or Encourage someone to speak: *Mario, I'd like to know your opinion about that*).

2   Brainstorm topics that they would be interested in talking about and ask them to choose one.

3   Ask students to work in groups of three or four and tell them they are going to have a conversation about the chosen topic but as they do, they will tick any of the things that they do (Ask a question, Clarify...). Their goal is to try to do all at some point during the conversation.

4   When they have had enough time to develop their conversations, stop them and ask each group to summarize their ideas on the topic discussed and then present these to the rest of the class.

Variation

You could make it a rule that in their group when they speak, they can't speak again until everyone else in the group has spoken. This helps keep participation equal.

Note

This is a variation of an activity used in cooperative learning; see Kagan (1994).

7.4 Talk, talk, talk

Give an idea

Respond to an idea

Ask a question

Answer a question

Express a doubt

Ask for clarification

Clarify

Encourage someone to speak

Make a positive comment about someone's idea

Agree

Disagree

Getting to know you

Focus	Writing: Introducing yourself and giving personal information
Level	Beginners to Lower intermediate
Time	30-40 minutes
Preparation	None

in class

1   A good deal of interaction is done on the internet so it can be useful to practise written interaction. Tell your students that they are going to write an e-mail giving their personal information. Provide them with basic structures to do this. Ask them to imagine they are writing to someone they don't know to introduce themselves for some purpose. You might suggest a few purposes that would be appropriate for your group.

2   When they have had time to finish, ask them to work in pairs and exchange their e-mails and answer them in writing as if they didn't know each other. They can write a few questions, comment on some things their partner has written and add some more of their own personal information.

3   Give students time to read their partner's answer and then ask the whole class if they learned anything interesting that they didn't know about their partner.

Advice from a tree

Focus Describing trees, giving advice
Level Lower intermediate and above
Time 30-40 minutes
Preparation Make copies or prepare a slide of the poem below; choose a problem from a magazine problem page and the reply from the "agony aunt" and make a copy for each group of three or four students.

in class

1 If there are any trees that can be seen from the classroom window, ask the students to choose one they like and to describe it. Alternatively, show pictures of trees and ask the students in pairs, to write down as many adjectives as possible to describe the trees.

2 Invite students to give you their adjectives and write them up on the board. Depending on the level taught, you might want to add a few of your own and explain their meanings. With higher level class you could give them a few idioms too. (See suggestions below.)

3 Now ask students which of the adjectives can also be used to describe people.

4 Tell them to reflect on the literal meaning as well as metaphorical (*straight*, for example).

5 Next, ask the students to imagine the tree they picked knows their situation at the moment and can give them advice on any difficulties they might have. What would it say? Students write this down in a short paragraph (*Be strong, Be wise,* etc.)

6 Invite a few pairs to share their contributions with the group.

7 Show the poem below on the screen, or hand out a copy to the students. Ask them if there are any similarities between what they wrote and the poem.

8 Give students a copy of the problem that someone wrote to an "agony aunt" about. Ask them to work in groups and discuss the situation of the writer and see what suggestions they would make. Each group gives their solution to the class and then you can read the solution given by the "agony aunt".

> **strong, leafy, tall, colourful, green, stout, massive, gnarled, straight, majestic, towering, ancient, rooted, shady**

> **Money doesn't grow on trees. Bark up the wrong tree.**
>
> **Can't see the forest for the trees. The tree is known by its fruit.**
>
> **Shake like a leaf. Turn over a new leaf.**

ADVICE FROM A TREE

Stand tall and proud
Sink your roots deeply into the earth
Reflect the light of your true nature
Think long term...

Go out on a limb
Remember your place among all living beings
Embrace with joy the changing seasons
For each yields its own abundance
The energy and birth of spring
The growth and contentment of summer
The wisdom to let go the leaves in the fall
The rest and quiet renewal of winter

Feel the wind and the sun
And delight in their presence
Look up at the moon that shines down upon you
And the mystery of the stars at night
Seek nourishment from the good things in life
Simple pleasures
Earth.. fresh air.. light
Be content with your natural beauty
Drink plenty of water
Let your limbs sway and dance in the breezes
Be flexible
Remember your roots.. and
Enjoy the view

By Ilan Sham

7.7

Reporters

Focus	Reporting what someone said
Level	Elementary and above
Time	35-40 minutes
Preparation	None

in class

1 Review how to express reported speech. Explain that if something is still true, you don't put what is reported in the past tense.

2 Put the students in groups of three and assign roles (A/B/C/).

3 Ask the As to say something true about themselves, just a short phrase. (e.g. *My name is Marie and I live in Paris*). The Bs pretend they did not hear very well and say something like: *She said her name's Valérie and she lives in London*. The Cs then say: *No, actually, she said her name's Marie and she lives in Paris*. The As carry on with a second phrase (*I live in an old apartment with my parents and my twin brother*). The Bs say: *She said she lives in a modern building by herself...* The Cs correct the Bs. And so on.

4 After a while, ask the students to change roles (e.g. the Bs start saying something about themselves, the Cs have the role the Bs had, and the As the Cs' role). Then a little later they change again and the Cs talk about themselves. This way everyone will get to do each task.

5 Finally, they change places with someone in another group and tell them something they learned about the other people in their original group.

Note

This can be a useful activity to do at the beginning of a course to help learners get to know something about each other.

7.8

When were you born?

Focus	Asking and answering *Where/When were you born? / I was born...*
Level	Lower intermediate and above
Time	25-30 minutes
Preparation	None

in class

1   Ask students to work in pairs. Student A asks Student B: '*Where were you born*'? Student B gives as many answers as possible (*I was born in Madrid. I was born in Spain. I was born in Europe. I was born in a big city,* etc.)

2   When the Bs have no more answers , the As ask: '*When were you born?* ' The Bs give as many answers as possible (*I was born in July. I was born in 1963. I was born in the summer, on a hot day, I was born at 2 a.m., I was born on a Saturday,* etc.).

3   The students then change roles: the B's ask the questions, and the A's answer.

4   Now ask students to comment on/ask additional questions on something that was said during the exchange. For example: *You said you were born in (Madrid). What was it like to live there?*

5   Each pair then works with another pair and each person gives the other pair some information they learned about their partner.

6   Next, invite the students to stand up, mingle and ask other classmates the same questions (*Where/When were you born?*), and as they do, specify something for them to try to find: two people in the group who were born in big cities/villages or the countryside, who have their birthdays in winter/summer months etc.

7   Finally, invite the students to report to the rest of class.

Note

This activity gives students the opportunity to interact in the target language and the repetition involved can help them to get control of the structure.

7.9

A future friend

Focus	Asking and answering questions related to opinions
Level	Lower intermediate and above
Time	30-40 minutes
Preparation	Make copies of the role-play cards for each student.

in class

1 Review the interrogative forms and ways to express opinions about activities (*I love swimming, I enjoy reading...*).

2 Tell students they are going to have a new identity and to find a new friend. Give each student a card with two things about their new self and two things about the person who is going to be their friend. If you have more students, prepare similar cards so each one has a different card. With an odd number of students, two can have the same card and three of them will be new friends.

3 They walk around the room asking their classmates questions related to the information about their future friend: *Do you enjoy reading mystery novels?... Did you study in Rome last summer?* They continue asking questions until they find the person with the matching card. They and their friend have to answer yes to both sets of questions.

4 When they find their friend, they imagine three years have passed and they prepare a short conversation about something that they did during the three years since they met.

5 Each pair says their conversation for the rest of the class

7.9 A future friend

YOUR FUTURE FRIEND: Your future friend loves swimming and skateboarding. Your future friend went to London with a cousin last year. --------------------------------- YOU: You often read romantic books. You lived in Paris when you were a child.	**YOUR FUTURE FRIEND:** Your future friend often reads romantic books. Your future friend lived in Paris when she was a child. --------------------------------- YOU: You love swimming and skateboarding. You went to London with your cousin last year
YOUR FUTURE FRIEND Your future friend likes swimming but he hates skateboarding. Your future friend travelled to Rome with his sister two years ago. --------------------------------- YOU: You were in London with your father three years ago. You usually go to the cinema with your friends.	**YOUR FUTURE FRIEND** Your future friend was in London with his father three years ago. Your future friend usually goes to the cinema with his friends. --------------------------------- YOU: You like swimming but you hate skateboarding. You travelled to Rome with your sister two years ago.

7.9 A future friend

YOUR FUTURE FRIEND	YOUR FUTURE FRIEND
Your future friend studied in Rome last summer.	Your future friend visited Paris with his brother two years ago.
Your future friend enjoys reading mystery novels.	Your future friend loves watching horror films.
--------------------------------	--------------------------------
YOU:	YOU:
You visited Paris with your brother two years ago.	You enjoy reading mystery novels.
You love watching horror films.	You studied in Rome last summer.
YOUR FUTURE FRIEND	YOUR FUTURE FRIEND
Your future friend enjoys writing mystery novels.	Your future friend loves jogging and going shopping
Your future friend worked in Dublin five years ago	Your future friend played the piano when he was six years old.
--------------------------------	--------------------------------
YOU:	YOU:
You love jogging and going shopping	You enjoy writing mystery novels.
You played the piano when you were six years old.	You worked in Dublin five years ago.

7.9 A future friend

YOUR FUTURE FRIEND	YOUR FUTURE FRIEND
Your future friend goes jogging twice a week.	Your future friend hates cooking and washing dishes.
Your future friend visited Berlin last year.	Your future friend mate studied in Sweden.
------------------------------------	------------------------------------
YOU:	YOU:
You hate cooking and washing dishes.	You go jogging twice a week.
You studied in Sweden.	You visited Berlin last year.
YOUR FUTURE FRIEND	YOUR FUTURE FRIEND
Your future friend goes fishing on Mondays	Your future friend prefers studying in the morning.
Your future friend lived in Norway last year.	Your future friend visited Brussels last year.
------------------------------------	------------------------------------
YOU:	YOU:
You prefer studying in the morning	You go fishing on Mondays.
You visited Brussels last year.	You lived in Norway last year.

Acknowledgement

This activity is a version of one by Laura Castillo.

7.10

Role-play with a twist

Focus	Listening and speaking: Noticing target language
Level	Lower intermediate and above
Time	30-35 minutes
Preparation	Choose a role play topic and a set of words/phrases you would like to highlight and which fit into the overall topic of the role play; write the selected words/phrases on the board.

in class

1   Ask students to work in groups (numbers depend on how many people there are in the role play) and tell them about the situation they will need to perform (e.g. TV debate between famous politicians; police interrogation of a suspect, etc.).

2   Ask them to prepare for an unscripted role-play performing the situation you have selected but with a difference: they will need to include each word/phrase on the board once, but one of them twice.

3   The groups perform their role plays and the rest of the class must spot the phrase that has been used twice.

Variation

A more difficult version is when students have to include all but one of the selected words/phrases, and the task for the rest of the class is to identify the missing item.

References

Celce-Murcia, M., Dörnyei, Z., & Thurrell, S. (1997). Direct approaches in L2 instruction: A turning point in communicative language teaching? *TESOL Quarterly, 31*, 141-152.

Celce-Murcia, M., Dörnyei, Z., & Thurrell, S. (1998). On directness in communicative language teaching. *TESOL Quarterly, 32*, 116-119.

Collentine, J. (2009). Study abroad research: Findings, implications and future directions. In C. J. Doughty & M. H. Long (Eds.), *The handbook of language teaching* (pp. 218-233). Oxford: Blackwell.

DeKeyser, R., & Criado, R. (2013a). Automatization, skill acquisition, and practice in second language acquisition. In C. A. Chapelle (Ed.), *The Encyclopedia of applied linguistics (on-line)* (pp. 1-8). Malden, MA: Wiley-Blackwell.

DeKeyser, R., & Criado, R. (2013b). Practice in second language instruction. In C. A. Chapelle (Ed.), *The Encyclopedia of applied linguistics (on-line)* (pp. 1-4). Malden, MA: Wiley-Blackwell.

Dörnyei, Z. (2009). *The psychology of second language acquisition*. Oxford: Oxford University Press.

Dörnyei, Z. (2013). Communicative language teaching in the twenty-first century: The 'Principled communicative approach'. In J. Arnold & T. Murphey (Eds.), *Meaningful action: Earl Stevick's influence on language teaching* (pp. 161-171). Cambridge: Cambridge University Press.

Dörnyei, Z., & Kubanyiova, M. (2014). *Motivating learners, motivating teachers: Building vision in the language classroom*. Cambridge: Cambridge University Press.

Ellis, R. (2008). *The study of second language acquisition* (2nd ed.). Oxford: Oxford University Press.

Frank, C., & Rinvolucri, M. (1991). *Grammar in action again: Awareness activities for language learning*. Hemel Hempstead: Prentice Hall.

Gatbonton, E., & Segalowitz, N. (2005). Rethinking communicative language teaching: A focus on access to fluency. *Canadian Modern Language Review, 61*(3), 325-353.

Hadfield, J., & Dörnyei, Z. (2013). *Motivating learners*. Harlow, England: Pearson.

Kagan, S. (1994). *Cooperative Learning*. 2nd ed. San Clemente, CA: Kagan Publishing.

Krashen, S. (1982). *Principles and practice in second language acquisition*. Oxford: Pergamon.

Lightbown, P. M., & Spada, N. (2006). *How languages are learned* (3rd ed.). Oxford: Oxford University Press.

Littlewood, W. (1981). *Communicative language teaching: An introduction*. Cambridge: Cambridge University Press.

Littlewood, W. (2011). Communicative language teaching: An expanding concept for a changing world. In E. Hinkel (Ed.), *Handbook of research in second language teaching and learning* (Vol. II, pp. 541-557). New York: Routledge.

Mackey, A., & Goo, J. (2013). Interaction approach in second language acquisition. In C. A. Chapelle (Ed.), *The encyclopedia of applied linguistics (on-line)* (pp. 1-10). Malden, MA: Wiley-Blackwell.

Markus, H., & Ruvolo, A. (1989). Possible selves: Personalized representations of goals.

References

In L. A. Pervin (Ed.), *Goal concepts in personality and social psychology* (pp. 211-241). Hillsdale, NJ: Lawrence Erlbaum.

MOSKOWITZ, G. (1978). *Caring and sharing in the foreign language classroom.* Newbury House.

PAIGE, R. M., COHEN, A. D., KAPPLER, B., CHI, J. C., & LASSEGARD, J. P. (2002). *Maximizing study abroad: A students' guide to strategies for language and culture learning and use.* Minneapolis, MN: Center for Advanced Research for Language Acquisition, University of Minnesota.

RANTA, L., & LYSTER, R. (2007). A cognitive approach to improving immersion students' oral language abilities: The Awareness-practice-feedback sequence. In R. M. DeKeyser (Ed.), *Practice in second language: Perspectives from applied linguistics and cognitive psychology* (pp. 141-160). New York: Cambridge University Press.

RATEY, J. (2008). *Spark.* New York: Little, Brown and Company.

RICHARDS, J. C., & RODGERS, T. S. (2001). *Approaches and methods in language teaching* (2nd ed.). Cambridge: Cambridge University Press.

ROBERTS, C., BYRAM, M., BARRO, A., JORDAN, S., & STREET, B. (2001). *Language learners as ethnographers.* Clevedon: Multilingual Matters.

ROGERS, C. R. (1965). *Client-centered therapy: Its current practice, implications, and theory.* Boston, MA: Houghton Mifflin.

SINCLAIR, J. (1991). *Corpus, concordance, collocation.* Oxford: Oxford University Press.

SPADA, N. (2007). Communicative language teaching: Current status and future prospects. In J. Cummins & C. Davison (Eds.), *International handbook of English language teaching* (Vol. 1, pp. 271-288). New York: Springer.

WIDDOWSON, H. G. (1989). Knowledge of language and ability for use. *Applied Linguistics, 10*, 128-137.

Further resources

What is the Principled Communicative Approach?

The theoretical basis of the Principle Communicative Approach is described in:
DÖRNYEI, Z. (2009). *The Psychology of second language acquisition.* Oxford: Oxford University Press.

A concise summary can be found in:
DÖRNYEI, Z. (2013). *Communicative language teaching in the twenty-first century: The 'Principled Communicative Approach'.* In J. Arnold & T. Murphey (Eds.), Meaningful Action: Earl Stevick's Influence on Language Teaching (pp. 161-171). Cambridge: Cambridge University Press.

Other relevant discussions of CLT in the 21st century include:
CELCE-MURCIA, M., DÖRNYEI, Z., & THURRELL, S. (1997). Direct approaches in L2 instruction: A turning point in communicative language teaching? TESOL Quarterly, 31, 141-152.

Further resources

LITTLEWOOD, W. (2011). *Communicative language teaching: An expanding concept for a changing world. In E. Hinkel (Ed.), Handbook of research in second language teaching and learning* (Vol. II, pp. 541-557). New York: Routledge.

SAVIGNON, S. J. (2007). Beyond communicative language teaching: What's ahead? *Journal of pragmatics*, 39, 207-220.

SPADA, N. (2007). *Communicative language teaching: Current status and future prospects. In J. Cummins & C. Davison (Eds.),* International handbook of English language teaching (Vol. 1, pp. 271-288). New York: Springer.

WHONG, M. (2012). *A linguistic perspective on communicative language teaching.* Language Learning Journal, 41(1), 115-128.

Chapter 1

A classic summary of student-centred learning is offered by:

ROGERS, C., & FREIBERG, H. J. (1994). *Freedom to learn (3rd ed.).* New Jersey: Prentice Hall.

A practical overview of student-centred learning can be found in:

BRANDES, D., & GINNIS, P. (1986). *A Guide to student-centred learning.* Oxford: Blackwell.

Some useful resource books containing personalised, student-centred L2 activities are:

GRIFFITHS, G., & KEOHANE, K. (2000). *Personalizing language learning.* Cambridge: Cambridge University Press.

MOSKOWITZ, G. (1978). *Caring and Sharing in the Foreign Language Classroom.* Newbury House.

PUCHTA, H., & RINVOLUCRI, M. (2007). *Multiple intelligences in EFL: Exercises for secondary and adult students.* Innsbruck: Helbling Languages.

Chapter 2

There has been a lot of research on the role of input in SLA. A good starting point might be a Special Issue of the *Modern Language Journal (93/3, 2009). This is the Editors' introduction:*

ELLIS, N., & COLLINS, L. (2009). *Input and second language acquisition: The roles of frequency, form, and function. Introduction to the special issue.* Modern Language Journal, 93(3), 329-335.

On explicit learning and the resulting explicit knowledge, see:

ERLAM, R. (2013). *Explicit knowledge and grammar explanation in second language instruction.* In C. A. Chapelle (Ed.), The Encyclopedia of applied linguistics (on-line) (pp. 1-5). Malden, MA: Wiley-Blackwell.

LEOW, R. P. (2007). Input in the 12 classroom: An attentional perspective on receptive practice. In R. M. DeKeyser (Ed.), *Practice in second language: Perspectives from applied linguistics and cognitive psychology (pp. 21-50).* New York: Cambridge University Press.

MUÑOZ, C. (2013). *Explicit learning in second language acquisition. In C. A. Chapelle (Ed.), The Encyclopedia of applied linguistics (on-line) (pp. 1-6).* Malden, MA: Wiley-Blackwell.

Further resources

Chapter 3

The following anthology offers an excellent introduction to skill learning theory and automatization in second language learning:

DeKeyser, R. M. (Ed.). (2007). *Practice in second language: Perspectives from applied linguistics and cognitive psychology.* New York: Cambridge University Press.

This chapter within this anthology is particularly relevant:

Ranta, L., & Lyster, R: *A cognitive approach to improving immersion students' oral language abilities: The Awareness-Practice-Feedback sequence* (pp. 141-160).

Further theoretical explanation is given by:

DeKeyser, R., & Criado, R. (2013). *Automatization, skill acquisition, and practice in second language acquisition. In C. A. Chapelle (Ed.), The Encyclopedia of applied linguistics (on-line)* (pp. 1-8). Malden, MA: Wiley-Blackwell.

DeKeyser, R., & Criado, R. (2013). *Practice in second language instruction. In C. A. Chapelle (Ed.), The Encyclopedia of applied linguistics (on-line)* (pp. 1-4). Malden, MA: Wiley-Blackwell.

Segalowitz, N. (2010). *Cognitive bases of second language fluency.* New York: Routledge

Practical suggestions are offered in:

Gatbonton, E., & Segalowitz, N. (1988). Creative automatization: Principles for promoting fluency within a communicative framework. *TESOL Quarterly*, 22(3), 473-492.

Gatbonton, E., & Segalowitz, N. (2005). Rethinking communicative language teaching: A focus on access to fluency. *Canadian modern language review*, 61(3), 325-353.

Chapter 4

The literature on focus on form and form-focused instruction is extensive, and there is also a wide range of teachers' resource books available on the communicative teaching of grammar. The following works offer a balanced theoretical overview:

Lowen, S. (2011). Focus on Form. In E. Hinkel (Ed.), *Handbook of research in second language teaching and learning (Vol. II, pp. 576-592).* New York: Routledge.

Nassaji, H., & Fotos, S. (2011). *Teaching grammar in second language classrooms: Integrating form-focused instruction in communicative context.* New York: Routledge

Ur, P. (2011). Grammar teaching. In E. Hinkel (Ed.), *Handbook of research in second language teaching and learning (Vol. II, pp. 507-522).* New York: Routledge.

Some useful teachers' resources:

Frank, C., & Rinvolucri, M. (1991). *Grammar in action again: Awareness activities for language learning.* Hemel Hempstead: Prentice Hall.

Gerngross, G., Puchta, H., & Thornbury, S. (2006). *Teaching grammar creatively.* Innsbruck: Helbling Languages.

Rinvolucri, M. (1984). *Grammar games: Cognitive, affective and drama activities for EFL Students.* Cambridge: Cambridge University Press.

Further resources

Chapter 5

The teaching of formulaic languages is an emerging new field. A good overview can be found in a Special Issue of the *Annual review of applied linguistics (Vol. 32, 2012)*, which contains 12 articles written by leading international experts. The following articles also offer useful insights:

ALALI, F. A., & SCHMITT, N. (2012). Teaching formulaic sequences: The same as or different from teaching single words? *TESOL Journal, 3(2)*, 153-180.

GATBONTON, E., & SEGALOWITZ, N. (2005). Rethinking communicative language teaching: A focus on access to fluency. *Canadian modern language review,* 61(3), 325-353.

SCHMITT, N. (2013). Formulaic language and collocation. In C. A. Chapelle (Ed.), *The Encyclopedia of applied linguistics (on-line) (pp. 1-10).* Malden, MA: Wiley-Blackwell.

A useful resource book:

LINDSTROMBERG, S., & BOERS, F. (2008). *Teaching chunks of language: From noticing to remembering.* Innsbruck: Helbling Languages.

Chapter 6

There is a wide range of materials focusing on reading and listening tasks. The following works offer theoretical insights into the implicit processes occurring during such activities.

HULSTIJN, J. H. (2013). Incidental learning in second language acquisition. In C. A. Chapelle (Ed.), *The encyclopedia of applied linguistics (on-line) (pp. 1-5).* Malden, MA: Wiley-Blackwell.

REBUSCHAT, P., & WILLIAMS, J. (2013). Implicit learning in second language acquisition. In C. A. Chapelle (Ed.), *The encyclopedia of applied linguistics (on-line) (pp. 1-7).* Malden, MA: Wiley-Blackwell.

SANZ, C., & LEOW, R. P. (EDS.). (2011). *Implicit and explicit language learning: Conditions, processes, and knowledge in SLA and bilingualism.* Washington, DC: Georgetown University Press.

Chapter 7

There is ample practical material available to engage learners in real or simulated communicative experiences. The following works offer good summaries of the rationale for placing emphasis on L2 interaction, including study abroad.

DEKEYSER, R. M. (2007). Study abroad as foreign language practice. In R. M. DeKeyser (Ed.), *Practice in second language: Perspectives from applied linguistics and cognitive psychology (pp. 208-226).* New York: Cambridge University Press.

MACKEY, A. (2007). Interaction as practice. In R. M. DeKeyser (Ed.), *Practice in second language: Perspectives from applied linguistics and cognitive psychology (pp. 85-110).* New York: Cambridge University Press.

MACKEY, A., ABBUHL, R., & GASS, S. (2012). Interactionist approaches. In S. Gass & A. Mackey (Eds.), *The routledge handbook of second language acquisition (pp. 7-23).* New York: Routledge.

Teacher's quick-reference guide

This guide will help you select an activity suitable for your class based on the time you have available and the learning level(s) of your students, and other factors such as the content and language focus.

To use it, look down the left-hand column under a particular chapter till you come to a time that's suitable for you, and then look across to see the name of the activity spread across the range of levels it's suited to. Then across again to to find the focus and the activity number.

If you prefer to start with the level of your students, find the level on the top line, then go downwards till you find an activity name, and on that same row you will find the time required, the content focus and language focus, and the activity number.

Please note that the guidance is very basic; it allows you to see, when you're thinking of running an activity for the first time, how long the activity is likely to take according to the authors' experience.

Teacher's quick-reference guide

Lesson time	Beginner	Elementary	Lower Intermediate	Intermediate	Upper Int	Focus	Activity number
Chapter 1							
25–30					What's in a poem	Personal responses to a poem	1.1
15–20			How would it be at home?			Comparing coursebook material to students' own lives	1.2
15–20			Routines			Adverbs of frequency with habits and routines	1.3
20–25		I'm good at this!				*I'm good at + -ing*	1.4
30–40			Read all about me			Life in the future	1.5
10–20 per day for presentations + 40 follow up			Your town, my town, our town			A presentation for visitors to your town	1.6
15–20 + 20–30	Personal strategies for learning					Developing personalized learning strategies	1.7
40–50			Goal + effort = success			Setting goals for learning	1.8
40–50			A conditional weekend			First conditional	1.9
15 + homework			Bring the past to the present			An account of someone's life in the past	1.10
25–30			What about you?			Expressing personal opinions	1.11
20–30			From the composer's point of view			Imagining how an artist feels about their creation	1.12
Chapter 2							
10–15	Signs					Classroom language	2.1
20–30	Thanks so much					Giving and receiving gifts	2.2
20–30	I am, it is					Adjectives with *-ed* and *-ing* endings	2.3
20–30			Be a detective			Making deductions	2.4
15–30	Degrees					Likes and dislikes	2.5
15–20		This song and that song				Comparatives	2.6
25–30			Dear friend			Reactions and opinions	2.7
20–25	Rote learning					Memorizing lyrics	2.8

Lesson time	Beginner	Elementary	Lower Intermediate	Intermediate	Upper Int	Focus	Activity number
30–45				Are you for or against it?		Discourse markers	2.9
15–20			You can say that again			Agreeing, using intensifiers	2.10
20–25			Pessimists, optimists			Agreeing and disagreeing	2.11

Chapter 3							
20--30			Did you know...?			*Did you know ... ?* questions	3.1
20--30			Not anymore!			Past habits, *used to*	3.2
30–40			Ever so simple			*Do you ever...? & Have you ever...?*	3.3
20–30			We were saying ...			Past continuous in reported speech	3.4
20–30			Is there anybody who ... ?			Queston forms	3.5
15–20		I can chant				Fluency and rhythm	3.6
20–30			Ha-ha-ha			Automatization of language; intonation	3.7
5-10		Inner workbench pronunciation				Pronunciation	3.8
10–15			Creative drills			Automatization of language	3.9
40–50			That is the question			Asking questions	3.10
15–20			Oh, by the way...			Breaking the ice: using chunks	3.11

Chapter 4							
20–30			It's all relative			Relative clauses	4.1
20–25				What has been done?		Passive	4.2
40–45			The right way			Polite language	4.3
10–15		Give me feedback				Asking for clarification and feedback	4.4
25–30			No one like you			Comparatives of equality	4.5
20–40		No one is perfect				Error correction	4.6
20–30			In the cloud			Past simple of irregular verbs	4.7
30–40			Special guest			Question formation	4.8

Teacher's quick-reference guide

Lesson time	Beginner	Elementary	Lower Intermediate	Intermediate	Upper Int	Focus	Activity number
30–40			My perfect future			Describing an ideal future life	4.9
10–15	Get physical!					Past simple and past participle of irregular verbs	4.10
10–15	Input to intake					Present simple and present continuous	4.11

Chapter 5

Lesson time	Beginner	Elementary	Lower Intermediate	Intermediate	Upper Int	Focus	Activity number
5–10	Shouting chunks					Learning chunks	5.1
25–30				Stories we tell		Revising chunks	5.2
20–25				Numbers and chunks		Reflecting on chunks	5.3
25–30			Finishing the chunk			Using chunks	5.4
10–15			Rating chunks			Reviewing chunks	5.5
10–15			Categories			Recycling chunks	5.6
10–15			Hold the phrase			Exploring language imaginatively	5.7
10–15	Speed it up					Memorizing chunks	5.8
30–40				Chunking on the walls		Chunks in context	5.9
30–40			Families of chunks			Chunks in real life situations	5.10
5–10 + 10–15				A pair of chunks		Matching chunks	5.11

Chapter 6

Lesson time	Beginner	Elementary	Lower Intermediate	Intermediate	Upper Int	Focus	Activity number
5–10			Getting ready for reading			Understanding main ideas	6.1
10–15			In the shadow			Listening comprehension and pronunciation	6.2
5–10 + homework	Sharing					Choosing authentic texts	6.3
10–15 + homework	Log in					Keeping a reading log	6.4
40–50	Walking the walls					Scanning for specific information	6.5
20–30				Mind the gaps		Noticing interesting language	6.6
5–10 + 20–25			I'll tell you			Retelling a story	6.7
15–25				Listening challenges		Listening for specific words and phrases	6.8

Lesson time	Beginner	Elementary	Lower Intermediate	Intermediate	Upper Int	Focus	Activity number
20–25			I hear you			Active listening	6.9

Chapter 7

Lesson time	Beginner	Elementary	Lower Intermediate	Intermediate	Upper Int	Focus	Activity number
20–25				My advice		Giving and receiving advice	7.1
20–25			Be a critic			Expressing opinions about a song	7.2
15–20 preparation + 2-3 per pair				Ring, ring		Making telephone calls	7.3
20–30			Talk, talk, talk			Conversational language	7.4
30–40	Getting to know you					Personal information	7.5
30–40		Advice from a tree				Describing trees; giving advice	7.6
35–40		Reporters				Reporting what someone said	7.7
25–30			When were you born?			Asking and answering questions (fact)	7.8
30–40			A future friend			Asking and answering questions (opinion)	7.9
30–35			Role-play with a twist			Noticing target language	7.10